EVERYDAY LIFE IN THE

ROMAN EMPIRE

KATHRYN HINDS

MARSHALL CAVENDISH
BENCHMARK BOOKS
NEW YORK

THE AUTHOR AND PUBLISHER WISH TO THANK J. BRETT MCCLAIN
OF THE ORIENTAL INSTITUTE OF THE UNIVERSITY OF CHICAGO
FOR HIS INVALUABLE HELP IN READING THE MANUSCRIPT.

MARSHALL CAVENDISH BENCHMARK 99 WHITE PLAINS ROAD TARRYTOWN, NEW YORK 10591
www.marshallcavendish.us   Text copyright © 2010 by Marshall Cavendish Corporation All rights reserved. No
part of this book may be reproduced or utilized in any form or by any means electronic or mechanical including
photocopying, recording, or by any information storage and retrieval system, without permission from the copyright holders. All Internet sites were available and accurate when this book was sent to press. LIBRARY OF
CONGRESS CATALOGING-IN-PUBLICATION DATA Hinds, Kathryn, 1962– Everyday life in the Roman Empire / by
Kathryn Hinds.   p. cm. Summary: "Provides a social history of life in the Roman Empire at its most powerful,
from 27 B.C.E. to 200 C.E., and includes descriptions of the ruling classes, the peasantry, and the urban
dwellers"–Provided by publisher.   ISBN 978-0-7614-4484-8 1.   Rome–History–Empire, 30 B.C. -284
A.D.–Juvenile literature.   2.   Rome–Social conditions–Juvenile literature.   3.   Rome–Social life and
customs–Juvenile literature.   4.   Social classes–Rome–Juvenile literature.   1.   Title.   DG276.5.H56 2010
937'.07–dc22   2009005913

EDITOR: JOYCE STANTON   PUBLISHER: MICHELLE BISSON
ART DIRECTOR: ANAHID HAMPARIAN   SERIES DESIGNER: MICHAEL NELSON

Printed in Malaysia
135642

Front cover: An ancient Roman fresco depicts three women preparing for a ceremony dedicated to the god Bacchus.

Title page: A bull, about to be sacrificed as an offering to the gods, is led to the altar.

Back cover: This young man lived in Egypt during the second century, when the country was under Roman rule.

CONTENTS

ABOUT THE ROMAN EMPIRE

When we think about the Roman Empire, we may picture chariot races, marble statues, and the towering walls of the Colosseum. But these images tell only part of the story. The rest of the tale revolves around the many different people—the emperors, senators, noblewomen, generals, foot soldiers, merchants, craftspeople, farmers, slaves, poets, priests, priestesses, and more—who contributed to the strength and vitality of ancient Rome.

Springtime is personified in a painting that adorned a wall in first-century Pompeii.

According to traditional accounts, the Romans founded their city in 753 B.C.E. At first, Rome was ruled by kings. Around the fifth century B.C.E., it became a republic, governed by a Senate, citizen assemblies, and elected officials. Under its republican governments, Rome steadily expanded its power. Through a combination of war and diplomacy, the city built on seven hills overlooking the Tiber River united all of Italy under its rule. It conquered Carthage in North Africa, Macedonia in northern Greece, and kingdoms to the east and west that had once been part of the great Greek Empire. By the end of the first century B.C.E., the Roman Republic was master of the entire Mediterranean world.

Even as its strength increased abroad, Rome was plagued by a series of civil wars at home. The turmoil ended in 31 B.C.E., when an ambitious young politician named Octavian defeated all rivals and became the sole ruler of Rome. Four years later, the Senate gave Octavian a new name, Augustus, along with control of the government, military, and religious affairs. Augustus became Rome's absolute ruler and first emperor.

Augustus and the emperors who followed him spread Roman rule to the edges of the known world. At its height, the Roman Empire reached all the way from Britain to Persia. It brought together an array of European, African, and Middle Eastern peoples, forming a vibrant multi-

Staged hunts, in which specially trained men confronted wild beasts, were extremely popular in ancient Rome.

A man sells bread on a street in this scene from everyday life in ancient Rome.

cultural society. During much of the empire's existence, its various ethnic and religious groups got along with remarkable tolerance and understanding—a model that can still inspire us today. The Romans' tremendous achievements in the arts, architecture, literature, law, and philosophy have also inspired and influenced people in Europe and the Americas for hundreds of years.

Now let's step back in time and meet the men, women, and children who lived in Rome during the first two centuries of the empire, from 27 B.C.E. to around 200 C.E. These people had many of the same joys and sorrows, hopes and fears that we do today, but their world was very different from ours. Forget about cell phones, computers, cars, and televisions. Welcome to life in the Roman Empire. . . .

A variety of systems of dating have been used by different cultures throughout history. Many historians now prefer to use B.C.E. (Before Common Era) and C.E. (Common Era) instead of B.C. (Before Christ) and A.D. (Anno Domini), out of respect for the diversity of the world's peoples. In this book, all dates are C.E. unless otherwise noted.

THE PATRICIANS

· I ·

THE MAN AT THE TOP

IT BECAME ESSENTIAL TO PEACE, THAT ALL POWER
SHOULD BE CENTERED IN ONE MAN.
—TACITUS, *HISTORIES*

The ancient Romans hated kings. They had learned their history lessons well: the last few kings who ruled Rome in its early days were foreigners whom later generations remembered as corrupt tyrants. After the overthrow of the royal house in 509 B.C.E., the Roman republic was set up so that no one person would be able to hold absolute power. Two consuls headed the government. They were elected for one-year terms and equally shared *imperium,* the authority to command troops and to interpret and carry out the law. The consuls also played the leading role in the Senate, the body that created new laws and handled the republic's finances and foreign relations. Senators were not elected. Once a man had served in an elected office, he automatically became a member of the Senate for life.

opposite:
Julius Caesar gained so much control over the government that many Romans were afraid he would make himself king.

Consuls and other government officials were chosen by assemblies that were open to all male Roman citizens—that is, free men who met certain other qualifications. Assemblies of male citizens also voted on whether or not to go to war and whether or not to pass the laws proposed by the Senate. When the assemblies officially met, they could not debate the issues they were deciding on. Before a vote was held, however, discussion often took place at unofficial meetings, which could also be attended by women, slaves, and foreigners.

Rome's republican government was not "of the people, by the people, and for the people" in the sense that we understand today. Only wealthy nobles—a small portion of the population—were in a position to take an active part in government and politics. These people cherished their freedom from one-man rule. Yet as Rome conquered more and more of the Mediterranean world, the republic became increasingly difficult to govern efficiently. And as Rome grew more powerful and wealthy, there were Roman politicians and generals who could not resist the temptation to acquire some of that wealth and power for themselves.

In 44 B.C.E. Julius Caesar, the victor in a brutal civil war that had threatened to destroy the republic, had himself declared dictator for life. In the past, the consuls had sometimes appointed a dictator to take absolute command of the army and government during an emergency—but the dictator's term only lasted six months. Caesar's move angered many senators, and a group of them murdered him—but they could not save the republic. After another fourteen years of civil war, Caesar's grandnephew and adopted son Octavian emerged victorious. In 27 B.C.E. the Senate gave him the title Augustus (meaning "revered" or "worthy of honor"), and he claimed that he had restored the republic. In reality, he alone now controlled Rome—and its empire.

IMPERIAL POWERS

Augustus, an extremely intelligent and diplomatic man, was careful not to make the mistake that had doomed Julius Caesar. Instead of proclaiming himself dictator or king, he took the title *princeps,* "first citizen." Operating within the framework that had upheld Rome for nearly five hundred years, he served as one of the two annually elected consuls. The old republican forms of government were carefully maintained. The Senate and assemblies still met, and the powers that Augustus wielded were clearly defined, not arbitrary.

The *princeps,* however, was so enormously wealthy and influential that over the course of many years he was able to acquire the powers of every important office in the Roman government. For nine years in a row Augustus was elected a consul. After this, he was given lifelong tribunician power—the power that, in the republic, had belonged to officials called tribunes—enabling him to veto any laws, elections, decrees of the Senate, or actions of other officials. The Senate also repeatedly voted Augustus control of the provinces of Egypt, Gaul (present-day France and Belgium), Spain, and Syria—the large, important provinces where most of Rome's military forces were stationed. In 12 B.C.E. he was even elected to the lifelong position of high priest of the Roman

First citizen Augustus wearing a toga, the age-old formal dress of all male Roman citizens

state religion. It is no wonder that, as the historian Dio Cassius wrote around 200 C.E., "Nothing . . . was done which did not please Augustus."

Some senators resented the new state of affairs. Most Romans, however, seemed glad to accept the rule of Augustus. People were tired of decades of civil war and were grateful to the *princeps* for bringing peace and prosperity back to Rome. They felt that the government was now far more stable and efficient, and much less corrupt, than it had been in the later years of the republic. Augustus further won the people's favor by such actions as beautifying the city of Rome, renovating its temples, improving its water supply, sponsoring free public entertainment, and lowering the price of grain. He gave land or money to all retiring soldiers, and several times distributed money from his personal funds, or grain bought with his own money, to hundreds of thousands of Roman commoners.

Augustus ruled the Roman Empire for some forty years, dying in 14 C.E. at the age of about seventy-six. He had made sure that his stepson Tiberius would succeed him as *princeps*: during Augustus's lifetime, the Senate had given Tiberius tribunician power and *imperium,* and he had successfully served in a number of military and administrative posts. As the heir of Augustus's wealth and a man experienced in public service, Tiberius was easily accepted as emperor. Strabo, a Greek historian writing during the reign of Tiberius, affirmed that "the Romans and their allies have never enjoyed such an abundance of peace and prosperity as that which Augustus Caesar provided from the time when he first assumed absolute power, and which his son and successor, Tiberius, is now providing."

By Tiberius's death in 37 C.E., it was clear that one-man rule was in Rome to stay. It had taken Augustus decades to accumulate his powers, and Tiberius had also gradually acquired his authority during years of training and government service. But Tiberius's successor, his great-nephew Gaius Caligula, became *princeps* without having held any office. Neverthe-less, the Senate voted him all the powers that had been held by Augustus and Tiberius, and so it was with the emperors who followed. The Senate and people of Rome had come to accept without question the emperors' power, in the words of Dio Cassius, "to make levies, to collect money, to declare war, to make peace, to rule foreigners and citizens alike, anytime, anywhere."

WORKING WITH THE SENATE

During Rome's centuries as a republic, the Senate had been supreme. Senators and their families made up the wealthiest and most privileged class in Roman society. Even as Augustus accumu-lated his powers of government, he was careful to maintain the best possible relationship with the Senate, since it represented the inter-ests of the wealthy and influential nobility. The highest government posts were still reserved for the senators. The Senate and its members also continued to deal with routine government business in Italy and in the provinces that were not under the emperor's direct control.

Augustus and Tiberius both made important changes in the Sen-ate's activities and procedures. Augustus tried to make the Senate a

top left:
Tiberius, the second emperor

top right:
Gaius Caligula, portrayed on a gold coin

A meeting of the Senate, as imagined by a nineteenth-century artist

more efficient body by decreasing its size from a thousand men to about six hundred. He also gave it a new role as a high court of law, hearing and judging cases of political importance (although some later emperors preferred to judge such cases themselves). In 5 B.C.E. Augustus set another pattern for the future by having two pairs of consuls elected every year, each pair serving a six-month term. Soon after coming to power, Tiberius did away with elections in the assemblies, which afterward met only for ceremonial purposes. From that time, all officials were elected by the Senate, and laws were passed by decrees of the Senate or edicts from the emperor.

The relationship between emperors and the Senate varied depending on circumstances and the people involved. Some emperors worked well with the Senate, while others—who were felt to seriously abuse their power—were hated by the Senate. Few senators could take the chance of standing up to the all-powerful emperor. At the same time, most emperors felt that it was wise not to offend the Senate, for they depended on senators to carry out many government functions. In any case, by the middle of the first century most senators had been nominated for office by the emperor himself. This meant that the Senate was largely filled with men loyal to the emperor (although they might not be so loyal to a succeeding emperor). The consuls and other officials had more prestige than real power. As the great Roman historian Tacitus put it, the senators had accepted the "futility of long speeches in the Senate, when the best men were quick to reach agreement elsewhere, and of endless haranguing of public meetings, when the final decisions were taken not by the ignorant multitude but by one man."

THE EMPEROR AND THE ARMY

Much of the emperor's power came from his control of the army. Early on, Augustus had taken an additional first name, *Imperator*—the source of our word "emperor"—meaning "commander in chief." (During the republic this had been a title granted to generals only temporarily, in honor of great victories.) By the seventies C.E., *Imperator* had become the usual title of the Roman ruler, highlighting his role as supreme military commander.

The imperial Roman army was made up of twenty-five to thirty-three units called legions, with around five thousand men in each. The legions were generally stationed along the empire's borders or in provinces where trouble was likely to arise. Auxiliaries—additional troops made up mostly of non-Roman citizens—supported the legions. Each legion was commanded by a legionary legate, a senator appointed by the emperor. A provincial governor—also chosen by the emperor—had military authority over all the legions stationed in his province. When there was fighting to be done in a province, it was generally the governor who took charge of the campaign as the emperor's representative.

A number of emperors led the army themselves. The emperor Trajan, for instance, waged three wars during his reign, adding to the empire Armenia, Mesopotamia, and Dacia, a large territory north of the Danube. Trajan was extremely popular with the army because he shared their dangers and hardships on campaign—and he seems to have genuinely enjoyed military life. Dio Cassius wrote, "Even if he did delight in war, nevertheless he was satisfied when success had been achieved, a most bitter foe overthrown and his countrymen exalted."

Sometimes when an emperor died and it was unclear who should succeed him, the army would declare one of its generals the new emperor. The army might even oust an emperor to replace him with its own candidate. During the year 69 C.E. this happened more than once. First the legions stationed in Germany revolted against the emperor Galba and proclaimed their commander, Vitellius, emperor. Galba was assassinated shortly afterward, and soldiers in the city of Rome declared another man emperor, Otho. A brief civil war ended in the death of Otho, but Vitellius's rule was not secure. The legions in Egypt and along the Danube River supported a new claimant to the throne, Vespasian, a popular general with an impressive service record. By the end of 69, Vespasian's forces were in control of Rome. Vespasian proved himself worthy of the army's faith in him, ruling the empire justly and wisely for ten years. The events of the year 69, however, proved an important point. Just as emperors controlled the Senate but also needed its support, so it was with the army: an emperor who did not have the army behind him was unlikely to stay in power for long.

⸙ THE FIRST TWENTY-ONE EMPERORS ⸙

Augustus, 27 B.C.E.–14 C.E.

Tiberius, 14–37

Gaius Caligula, 37–41

Claudius, 41–54

Nero, 54–68

Galba, 68–69

Otho, 69

Vitellius, 69

Vespasian, 69–79

Titus, 79–81

Domitian, 81–96

Nerva, 96–98

Trajan, 98–117

Hadrian, 117–138

Antoninus Pius, 138–161

Marcus Aurelius, 161–180

Lucius Verus, co-emperor with Marcus Aurelius 161–169

Commodus, co-emperor with Marcus Aurelius 178–180, sole emperor to 193

Pertinax, 193

Didius Julianus, 193

Septimius Severus, 193–211

Vespasian, 69–79

Augustus, 27 B.C.E.– 14 C.E.

II

MONUMENTS
TO POWER

BUT WHEN IT COMES TO PUBLIC BUILDING,
YOU DO IT ON A GRAND SCALE.
—PLINY THE YOUNGER, *PANEGYRIC*
(PRAISING THE EMPEROR TRAJAN)

From the time of Augustus—who made a famous declaration that he had found Rome a city of brick and left it a city of marble—nearly every emperor sponsored impressive building projects. Augustus himself had eighty-two temples restored in a single year. That was just the tip of the iceberg. Along with members of his family and court, the *princeps* gave the city of Rome countless other new and renovated structures, from government buildings to bathhouses and theaters, along with bridges, aqueducts, and roads. It was not just Rome that benefitted from the emperors' construction programs—the rest of Italy, and the provinces, too, received aqueducts, roads, and impressive buildings and monuments of many kinds.

opposite:
A temple built in what is now southern France during the reign of Augustus

18

PALACES AND PLEASURE GARDENS

Augustus preferred to live fairly simply, or at least no more luxuriously than other upper-class Romans. Since he did not want to be seen as a king, he did not live in a palace but in a regular house. It was not especially elegant—marble was used nowhere in the house, nor were there any mosaic floors. There were, however, wall paintings, which were common in all upper-class Roman homes. And at his summer house on the island of Capri, he displayed his collections of fossils and ancient weapons.

Few of the emperors who came after Augustus shared his simple tastes. Tiberius built an imperial residence on Rome's Palatine Hill; it is from *Palatine* that we get the word "palace." Many later emperors lived in the palace built for Domitian on top of the Palatine (completed in 92). Everything about Domitian's palace was designed to impress people with the emperor's might. The walls of the entryway were ninety-eight feet high, the audience hall or throne room was gigantic, and the dining room used for state banquets was almost as large. These rooms were decorated with huge statues, rich wall paintings, and marble (in thin sheets on both walls and floors) in a wide range of colors, imported from all over the empire. The private apartments, where the imperial family lived, were just as splendid. Domitian's palace also featured a curved, two-story covered walkway along the south side of the building; four courtyards (one with a fountain surrounded by an octagonal maze); and a huge sunken garden in the shape of a racetrack.

Nearly every emperor also had several residences outside the city of Rome—villas in the countryside, summer houses by the sea. The most famous and elaborate of all these retreats was the emperor Hadrian's villa in Tivoli, about fifteen miles east of Rome.

A portion of the artistic landscaping at the emperor Hadrian's villa in Tivoli

Hadrian, who ruled from 117 to 138, was an amateur architect and designed much of the villa himself. It took ten years to construct the buildings and landscape the grounds. When the complex was finished, it was nearly one-tenth the size of the city of Rome. Along with a palace, the estate included temples, bathhouses, guest-houses, banquet halls, two libraries, a theater, a swimming pool, an art gallery, and acres and acres of gardens. There were quarters for numerous servants and guards, underground service passages, and kitchens where food could be prepared for hundreds of people at once. The crown jewel of Tivoli was the emperor's personal retreat, an elegant house on a small island surrounded by a canal, which was in turn encircled by columns and statues; the whole retreat was enclosed by a high circular wall. The only way to the island was across a single bridge, which the emperor could even remove when he especially wanted to be left alone.

BUILDING TO PLEASE THE PEOPLE

Hadrian, like most emperors, did not build just for his own pleasure. He traveled throughout the empire, visiting thirty-eight of the

The Pantheon has been turned into a Christian church, but in most ways it looks the same today as it did during the reign of Hadrian.

empire's forty-four provinces. The *Augustan Histories** tell us that "in almost every city he constructed some building." In Rome itself Hadrian restored many monuments and rebuilt the Pantheon, a temple originally dedicated to all the gods. He may have taken part in the groundbreaking design of the Pantheon's lofty concrete dome, which was crowned by a circular opening, thirty feet across, that allowed sunlight to fill the temple's interior.

Emperors restored and built temples to beautify the empire and to glorify Rome (represented by the gods of the state)—and to show off their magnificence and generosity. Good public relations was one of the main reasons that emperors also sponsored the building of bathhouses, not only in Rome but in cities throughout the empire. Indoor plumbing was a rarity in the ancient world—it might be available in palaces and mansions, but that was it. To get clean, the majority of people in the empire's cities had to rely on the public baths. Along with bathing facilities, the great baths constructed by various emperors also offered swimming pools, gymnasiums, snack shops, libraries, meeting rooms, and pleasure gardens. They were all-purpose fitness and social centers, and Roman city dwellers were grateful to the emperors for providing them. From time to time emperors even paid all bathers' admission fees for a day, a week, or even a month.

*Also called *Historia Augusta* or *Writers of Augustan History,* this was a late fourth-century collection of biographies of Roman emperors.

A nineteenth-century artist made this painting of the ruins of a pool in a bathing complex in Roman Britain.

The public baths were places where people of different social classes mingled, and so were the amphitheaters. These huge structures were the scenes of open-air spectacles or entertainments that were held on holidays and other special occasions. One of the most famous buildings in the world is the Colosseum, the amphitheater begun in Rome by the emperor Vespasian. With terraced seating for more than 50,000 spectators, it was dedicated in 80 C.E. by Vespasian's son and successor, Titus. To celebrate the opening of the amphitheater, Titus sponsored one hundred days of gladiator combats and wild-animal fights.

Emperors also sponsored—and attended—chariot races in Rome's ancient racetrack, the Circus Maximus. Free spectacles and entertainments helped keep the city's people content by getting them out of their cramped apartments and distracting them from their problems. In the amphitheater, the circus, and the theater, the common people also had a chance to see their emperor and even, within certain limits, to express their honest opinions about various issues. It was worth an emperor's while to appear generous and

A Roman mosaic depicts a group of musicians entertaining the public.

accessible to the people, who might otherwise riot. As the teacher and orator Fronto wrote of the emperor Trajan,

> Because of his shrewd understanding . . . , the emperor gave his attention even to actors and other performers on stage or on the race track or in the arena, since he knew that the Roman people are held in control principally by two things— free grain and shows—that political support depends as much on the entertainments as on matters of serious import, that . . . neglect of the entertainments brings damaging unpopularity, . . . [and that] the shows placate everyone.

Along with understanding the importance of keeping the people of Rome entertained, Trajan enthusiastically promoted public works projects. He was responsible for paving many roads and building bridges throughout Italy. He had new harbor facilities constructed at Ostia, Rome's seaport. In the city of Rome itself he built an aqueduct (for bringing fresh water down from the mountains), an amphitheater especially for mock sea battles, a public

THE EMPEROR'S IMAGE

Thanks to television, newspapers, magazines, and the Internet, our leaders are familiar faces to us. The Roman emperors also wanted their faces to be familiar to the people they governed, but they had no mass media to rely on. They had to find other means, one of which was sculpture. Every emperor had himself portrayed in marble (and sometimes in bronze)—in full-length statues, in portrait busts, in reliefs carved on buildings and monuments. Statues and busts were sent out to all parts of the empire. A single emperor's statues might portray him in a variety of ways, some of them chosen to suit specific parts of the empire: the great conqueror, the divine ruler, the philosophical thinker, the bearer of the burdens of government.

Money made the emperors' faces even more familiar to the people of the empire, for every emperor issued coins with his portrait on them. On one side of the coin the emperor was seen in profile, often with an inscription giving some or all of his titles (emperors had so many titles that they usually had to be abbreviated). The other side of the coin gave the emperor the opportunity to express a message to the people. The design might include a deity that was important to the emperor or a personification of a particular virtue or quality, such as Victory or Discipline. Other designs on coins referred in words or pictures to specific achievements, such as conquests and building programs. Some emperors used their coins to really get their message across: some of Hadrian's coins, for instance, refer to him as "the enricher of the world."

Augustus, with the words *father of the country,* on a gold coin

bath, and a multistory semicircular marketplace with room for around 170 shops, storehouses, and offices. Trajan's Market was designed by the emperor's favorite architect, Apollodorus of Damascus—one of the most admired architects in the ancient world. Apollodorus also created Trajan's Forum, the largest and grandest public meeting place in Rome, beautifully ornamented with gilded statues and marble in many colors.

EMBLEMS OF IMPERIAL MIGHT

The achievements of emperors were often honored by special monuments, such as triumphal arches. Built of stone, these imposing structures usually featured sculpted reliefs that celebrated an emperor's military victories. Some emperors had columns erected to honor their conquests. The most famous of these is Trajan's Column, which is still standing on its original site in Trajan's Forum (in ancient times, there was a library on either side of the column). One hundred feet tall, it was made from twenty huge blocks of marble and originally had a statue of the emperor on top. The entire surface was covered with reliefs illustrating Trajan's conquest of Dacia (modern Romania). This visual record begins at the bottom of the column and spirals upward in twenty-three bands of sculpted pictures that can be "read" almost like a wordless comic strip.

A different kind of military monument was built by Trajan's successor, Hadrian. On a visit to the province

Scenes of conquest cover every inch of Trajan's Column.

of Britannia (Britain) in 122, the emperor ordered the building of a stone wall across what is now northern England to protect the Roman territory south of the wall from raids by tribes living in what is now Scotland. The wall was about seventy-six miles long, eight to ten feet thick, and took nearly ten years to build. It was fortified by lookout towers and milecastles, small forts roughly a mile apart, plus several larger fortresses. Hadrian's successor, Antoninus Pius, pushed Roman rule northward and had a thirty-six-mile-long earthen wall built at the new boundary. After about ten years, though, the Antonine Wall was abandoned, and Hadrian's Wall once more marked the northernmost limit of the Roman Empire.

opposite: Trajan's Column, today crowned with a statue of a Christian saint. The inside of the column is hollow; a spiral staircase with 185 marble steps leads up to the platform at the top.

III

THE IMPERIAL COURT

HIS FRIENDS HE ENRICHED GREATLY, EVEN THOUGH THEY DID NOT
ASK IT, WHILE TO THOSE WHO DID ASK, HE REFUSED NOTHING.
AND YET HE WAS ALWAYS READY TO LISTEN
TO WHISPERS ABOUT HIS FRIENDS.
—AUGUSTAN HISTORIES, LIFE OF HADRIAN

opposite:
The emperor
Vespasian
(right) greets
his son Domitian
(center), who is
attended by a
courtier. The
figures behind
them represent
the geniuses, or
spirits, of the
Senate and the
Roman people.

The emperor's court was wherever he was. Some emperors, such as Antoninus Pius, rarely left the city of Rome. Marcus Aurelius, on the other hand, spent five years of his reign in military camps along the Danube River, waging war against Germanic tribes that threatened the empire's borders. Then there was Hadrian, whose travels throughout the empire occupied a total of twelve years of his twenty-one-year reign.

In general, whether an emperor was at home in the palace, out leading the army, or visiting the provinces, he continued to mind the empire's business. He was the supreme judge in all legal cases involving Roman citizens—the final court of appeal. Foreign policy was his responsibility, and he met with ambassadors to discuss

border issues, trade agreements, and the like. Much of his time was spent on correspondence, for he had to supervise and advise provincial governors and other officials all over the empire. And of course, he was commander in chief of the military. Naturally, the emperor's court was filled with men of many ranks who assisted him in his various duties.

THE EMPEROR'S FRIENDS

The emperor generally had an informal council made up of men whom he knew well and trusted. Such men did not usually live at court but were summoned when the emperor wanted to discuss important issues and decisions with them. Because of their experience and good judgment, he could turn to them for reliable advice. These friends and supporters were most often senators, but sometimes they belonged to the next-highest Roman rank, the *equites,* or equestrians. An important member of Augustus's court, for example, was the equestrian Maecenas. He was also a well-known patron of literature, and through him some of Rome's greatest poets became part of the emperor's circle.

Writers in fact belonged to the courts of a number of emperors. At the beginning of Nero's reign, one of his top advisers was the playwright and philosopher Seneca the Younger. Later Nero chose the novelist Petronius as, in the words of Tacitus, "one of his few intimate associates, as a critic in matters of taste, while the emperor thought nothing charming or elegant in luxury unless Petronius had expressed to him his approval of it." Suetonius, who wrote biographies of emperors and other illustrious men, was chief librarian and palace secretary to Trajan. He continued in this position for a time under Hadrian, but after a few years he was dis-

THE PRINCEPS AND THE POETS

Virgil with two Muses

Augustus's good friend Maecenas loved poetry. He was an amateur poet himself, but his real gift was in recognizing and encouraging the talent of others. He gave generous financial support to such men and even brought them to the emperor's attention. Virgil, Horace, and Propertius—three of Rome's greatest poets—were all patronized by Maecenas and Augustus.

Maecenas suggested to each of these three that they write an epic celebrating the *princeps*'s achievements. Propertius responded with a witty poem in which he listed the deeds of Augustus that he would have included in an epic if he had been able to compose such a long, heroic poem—but after all, he concluded, he was really best at writing love poetry. Horace had also declared that he was not an epic poet, but he did write a number of shorter poems that praised Augustus. Virgil, however, early on promised that someday he would indeed write an epic. When he did, he produced one of the finest works of Latin literature, *The Aeneid*. And although the subject of the poem was Augustus's legendary heroic ancestor Aeneas, and not the *princeps* himself, Virgil still managed to glorify Augustus in a way that satisfied everyone.

Then there was Ovid, Rome's most popular poet during the reign of Augustus. Ovid had little or no contact with the court, yet the emperor couldn't help but notice him. Ovid was witty and irreverent, and he wrote many poems that poked fun at or flaunted the strict, old-fashioned values that Augustus promoted. The emperor was not amused. Even though Ovid ended his great, epic-length mythological poem *Metamorphoses* with Julius Caesar's transformation into a god, Augustus must have felt that most of Ovid's poetry was extremely immoral. Eventually the emperor sent him into exile, where he spent the rest of his life because of, as Ovid himself said, "a poem and a mistake."

~ OVID ON LOVE ~

Ovid's long poem *The Art of Love* is full of sly and witty advice about how to carry on a secret romance. In this selection, the poet suggests ways to make the most of a visit to the racetrack.

Don't neglect the horse races if you're looking for a place to meet your girlfriend. A circus crowded with people offers many advantages. You don't have to use a secret sign language here or be content with a slight nod to acknowledge one another's presence. Sit right next to your girlfriend—no one will stop you— and squeeze up beside her as closely as possible. It's really easy to do. The narrowness of each seating space forces you to squeeze together; in fact the rules for seating compel you to touch her!

Conversation should begin with no problem; just start out with the same comments that everyone else is making. Be sure to ask with great interest which horses are running and then immediately cheer for the same one, whichever it is, that she cheers for. . . .

Take advantage of every opportunity. If her skirt is trailing too far along the ground, pick up the edge of it and carefully lift the soiled part off the dust. At once you'll receive a reward for your careful concern; you'll be able to look at her legs, and she won't mind.

In addition, turn to whoever is sitting behind her and ask him not to jab her in the back with his knees. These little touches win over simple female hearts. Many men have found it useful to bring along a cushion which they can offer. It's also helpful to fan her with the racing program and to give her a stool for her dainty feet. Yes, the circus provides many opportunities for initiating a love affair.

missed for being disrespectful to the empress. Among Hadrian's friends and courtiers were philosophers, musicians, poets, mathematicians, and others. Galen, a man of many talents, served the emperors Marcus Aurelius, Commodus, and Septimius Severus as imperial physician. Galen also wrote works on philosophy, literature, grammar and, especially, medicine—in fact, his medical writings went on to become the standard textbooks for doctors throughout medieval Europe.

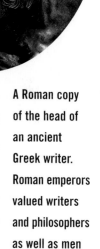

A Roman copy of the head of an ancient Greek writer. Roman emperors valued writers and philosophers as well as men of action.

Naturally, men of action often played a prominent role at court. For example, Augustus's closest friend and adviser was Marcus Agrippa, a skilled general. He was born a plebeian, or commoner, but through his own skill and intelligence rose to great influence. He supported and fought for Augustus during the civil wars, and afterward held many important government posts. He also founded the city of Cologne, Germany, as a settlement for retiring soldiers, and sponsored a number of important building projects in Rome. Augustus showed his great regard for Agrippa by giving the general his only child, Julia, in marriage.

THE PRAETORIAN GUARD

The emperor's bodyguard played a very important role at court. Known as the Praetorian Guard, for most of the first two centuries of the empire it numbered around five thousand men. Praetorian soldiers took turns at guard duty in the imperial palace (receiving the watchword from the emperor himself) and protected the emperor wherever he went. If the emperor went to war, usually the

The Praetorian Guard not only protected the emperor at court, but also accompanied him in battle.

whole Praetorian Guard accompanied him—they were an elite fighting force as well as a bodyguard.

Unlike soldiers in the legions, who were recruited from all over the Roman world, nearly all the Praetorians came from Italy. From the reign of Tiberius on, they were stationed in a camp on the northeast edge of Rome. Each member of the guard was required to serve for twelve years (later increased to sixteen). The Praetorians were the highest-paid soldiers in the empire, and they often received bonus payments from the emperors. Their special uniforms—with shining breastplates, plumed helmets, and oval shields—also set them apart from ordinary Roman soldiers.

The imperial bodyguard was commanded by an officer called the Praetorian prefect. He was chosen by the emperor from among the equestrians—this was one of the two top positions that men from that class could fill. (The other top post for *equites* was governor of Egypt, also appointed by the emperor.) Many ambitious equestrians strove for the emperor's recognition in the hope of someday becoming Praetorian prefect. A man who reached this goal could enjoy immense power and influence. For instance, Tiberius's Praetorian prefect Sejanus virtually ruled the empire for five years while the emperor lived in semiretirement on the island of Capri.

The Praetorian Guard sometimes was more interested in protecting its own interests than in protecting an emperor. The

A CRAFTY COURTIER

Some emperors could be easily swayed or deceived by the flattery and cunning of their courtiers. Tiberius placed perfect trust in his energetic and efficient Praetorian prefect, Sejanus, honoring him by making him a senator and a consul. The emperor became so reliant on Sejanus that he referred to him as "my partner in toil." But, as the historian Tacitus described him, Sejanus was not the loyal, upright subject he appeared to be:

> He won the heart of Tiberius so effectually by various artifices that the emperor, ever dark and mysterious towards others, was with Sejanus alone careless and freespoken. . . . He had a body which could endure hardships, and a daring spirit. He was one who screened himself, while he was attacking others; he was as cringing as he was imperious; before the world he affected humility; in his heart he lusted after supremacy, for the sake of which he was sometimes lavish and luxurious, but oftener energetic and watchful, qualities quite as mischievous when hypocritically assumed for the attainment of sovereignty.

Eventually Sejanus's deeds caught up with him. He had been responsible for murdering or exiling several members of the imperial family, including the men who were most likely to succeed Tiberius. Although Sejanus controlled all access to the emperor, who was living in seclusion on the island of Capri, Tiberius's sister-in-law Antonia managed to get a letter to him. She warned him about the Praetorian prefect's plans to rule the empire himself, and Tiberius at last became suspicious. The emperor secretly selected a new Praetorian prefect and gave him orders to arrest and kill Sejanus, whose ambitions ended in ruin.

Praetorians might fail to support a new emperor who did not pay them a bonus at the beginning of his reign. Several emperors who abused their power were murdered by members of the guard. The Praetorian Guard could also play a role in selecting a new emperor when there was no clear successor. Most famously, after Praetorian officers assassinated Gaius Caligula, they found his uncle Claudius hiding behind a curtain in the palace. The soldiers whisked him away to the Praetorian camp and proclaimed him emperor. With their loyalty sealed by huge bribes, members of the Senate were forced to accept the Praetorians' choice and voted to give Claudius all the privileges and powers of emperor.

SLAVES AND FREEDMEN

The imperial household included hundreds of slaves. Many of them performed the physical work of cleaning the palace, maintaining the gardens, laundering the emperor's togas, and so on. There were also skilled, highly trained slaves, such as cooks, physicians, and secretaries. Entertainers, both women and men, who lived at or visited the emperor's court were generally slaves, too. Among the slaves who took care of the emperor's personal needs were masseurs, barbers, and bedroom attendants (whose duties included making the bed, emptying and cleaning the chamber pot, and laying out the emperor's clothes for the day). Female slaves also lived in the palace to perform similar tasks for the women of the emperor's family.

Slaves who did their jobs well were often rewarded with their freedom. They still owed service and loyalty to the emperor, however, and often continued in their former jobs. Much of the day-to-day work of government administration was done by the imperial household's slaves and freedmen. Many were involved in keeping records and accounts and in writing up the emperor's correspondence. Some had very specialized jobs, such as the *nomenclator,* a kind of herald whose job was to announce the name of each person who came to visit the emperor.

The emperor's personal attendants had more contact with him than almost anyone else did. Naturally a closeness often developed between the emperor and these servants. He might confide in them and ask them for their advice. Because of their personal connection, these men could be quite influential, becoming close advisers of the emperor. Claudius was especially well known for relying on his freedmen and entrusting them with government matters. He especially favored his chief secretary, Narcissus, and his financial secretary, Pallas. The historian Suetonius recorded that Claudius "willingly permitted" Narcissus and Pallas to be

A slave carries a tray of food in preparation for a banquet.

> honoured by a decree of the Senate . . . with huge financial rewards . . . ; and he also allowed them to acquire such wealth legally and illegally that one day when he was complaining of a shortage of funds, someone answered quite wittily that he would have plenty if his two freedmen made him a partner.

IV

A MAN'S WORLD

THERE CAN BE GREAT MEN EVEN UNDER BAD EMPERORS, AND DUTY
AND DISCRETION, IF COUPLED WITH ENERGY OF CHARACTER AND A
CAREER OF ACTION, WILL BRING A MAN TO . . . GLORIOUS SUMMITS.
—TACITUS, *THE LIFE OF AGRICOLA*

Men in Rome's upper class shared a common culture and common expectations of life. Their careers revolved around the law, the army, and public office. These were leadership roles, and required men to be excellent communicators—arguing court cases, issuing orders, giving speeches, writing letters and reports. Skill in the use of language was a sign of success in the Roman world—and any man who wanted to be a success had to have that skill. Wealth was also very helpful. In the top level of society, men were expected to lay out large sums of money to fund building projects, provide entertainments, assist the poor, and the like. This helped forge strong bonds between the upper class and the common people, at least in the cities. This is one reason that

Roman society remained fairly stable during the first two centuries of the empire.

THE FIRST CITIZEN

The everyday business of the empire required the emperor to spend much of his time reading and writing letters, and composing, delivering, or listening to speeches. Some emperors were famous for multitasking: Augustus would dictate letters while being shaved or having his hair cut. The *Augustan Histories* remarked that Hadrian "wrote, dictated, listened, and, incredible as it seems, conversed with his friends, all at one and the same time." Emperors generally also attended meetings in the Senate House on a regular basis and sat in judgment at trials.

Of course, work did not take up all of an emperor's time. Like everyone else, an emperor had to eat, and dinner was often an occasion for enjoying a banquet and entertainment. Bathing, too, occupied an important place in nearly every Roman's day. Although the palace had its own bath facilities, some emperors, such as Titus and Hadrian, were singled out for praise because they "often bathed in the public baths, even with the common crowd."

As we have already seen, emperors also mingled with "the common crowd" in the theater, amphitheater, and circus. Some of Rome's rulers were not willing to be just spectators, however. Commodus shocked the Senate and common people alike by fighting as a gladiator in the arena. Gaius Caligula was so fond of chariot racing that he gave his favorite racehorse, Incitatus, "a stall of marble, a manger of ivory, purple blankets and a collar of precious stones, . . . a house, a troop of slaves and furniture"; he even invited Incitatus

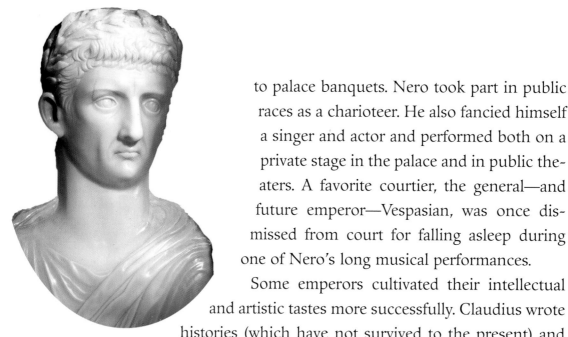

Claudius was a scholarly man, both before and after becoming emperor.

to palace banquets. Nero took part in public races as a charioteer. He also fancied himself a singer and actor and performed both on a private stage in the palace and in public theaters. A favorite courtier, the general—and future emperor—Vespasian, was once dismissed from court for falling asleep during one of Nero's long musical performances.

Some emperors cultivated their intellectual and artistic tastes more successfully. Claudius wrote histories (which have not survived to the present) and invented three new letters of the alphabet. Marcus Aurelius was a philosopher; his *Meditations,* written in Greek, is still a classic. Hadrian was the most wide-ranging of all in his interests and talents: he was said to be an expert in painting, arithmetic, geometry, and astrology; he sang, played the flute, and wrote poetry; and he enjoyed taking part in philosophical and literary debates. At the same time he was extremely fond of hunting and was skilled in the use of a wide variety of weapons.

THE LADDER OF SUCCESS

Hadrian, like a number of other emperors, began his career in the same manner as other highborn Roman males. He joined the army at the age of fifteen, then three years later was appointed to sit on a ten-judge panel that decided on matters of inheritance. After serving on this court, he received his first posting as a military tribune. This meant that he was second-in-command of a legion, working with the legate, or commander, and handling much of the legion's legal business. Hadrian was tribune of two different legions in turn (stationed first in what is now Hungary, then in what is now Bulgaria), before taking his first public office as quaestor.

Numerous quaestors served at once, playing various administrative and financial roles in the empire. They were involved in record keeping, worked in the treasury, and handled financial matters for provincial governors and generals in the field. Once a man had been quaestor, he automatically became a member of the Senate.

In the typical senator's career, the office of quaestor was followed by that of praetor. Praetors were judges in cases of civil law and also had responsibilities involving festivals and public games. An ex-praetor was eligible to be appointed as a legionary legate, a post he usually held for three or four years. After this he could spend a year as governor of one of the lesser provinces under the Senate's control. Then, if he had the emperor's favor, he would

✤ A ROUTINE DAY FOR THE EMPEROR ✥

Like most upper-class Romans, emperors often enjoyed a leisurely pace in their daily lives. This was true even of the emperors who took their responsibilities most seriously, such as Vespasian. The historian Suetonius describes for us Vespasian's "daily routine while emperor":

"He rose early, even while it was still dark. Then, after reading his letters and abstracts of official reports, he let in his friends, and while they chatted to him put on his shoes himself and got dressed. When he had dealt with any business that cropped up, he would find time for a drive and then a lie down. . . . After that he had a bath and then went through to dinner; it is said that he was at his most approachable and amenable at that time, so his household were eager to seize the opportunity of asking him something then."

An artist's reconstruction of the palace of the Roman governor of Britain, who had his headquarters in London

generally be put in charge of one of the emperor's provinces—but not one where more than a single legion was stationed.

The next step up the ladder was consul—as always, with the emperor's approval. Although consuls had very little power or responsibility under the emperors, most senators still found it an honor to hold the office. After a man had served as consul, the Senate might appoint him to a one-year term as governor of Africa (modern Tunisia and northwestern Libya) or Asia (today western Turkey), the greatest provinces under the Senate's control. Or the emperor could send him to govern a province with two or more legions, and he would stay in this office for as long as the emperor wished. Gnaeus Julius Agricola (father-in-law of the historian Tacitus) was governor of the province of Britain for seven or eight years, a fairly long time.

Between these various posts, many of which took him to the provinces, a man would spend periods at home in Rome, participating in the meetings of the Senate. He might also practice law, but senators were not allowed to engage in business. They could, however, invest in real estate, merchant expeditions, and similar moneymaking enterprises. Quite a few senators—among them the historians Tacitus and Dio Cassius—also devoted a good portion of their time to literature.

MANLY VIRTUES AND THE MILITARY

From the time of the early republic, noble Roman men were expected to live up to certain standards. Their highest calling was to serve the state, in both war and peace. The greatest virtues they could have, therefore, were *gravitas, pietas,* and *virtus.* These Latin words stood for concepts that were somewhat different from the meanings of the modern English words ("gravity," "piety," and "virtue") that descend from them. *Gravitas* basically meant "dignity," or "seriousness," and Roman noblemen and rulers were generally concerned about behaving in as dignified a manner as possible, which would inspire the respect of others. *Pietas* referred to properly doing one's duty to parents, country, and the gods. *Virtus* comes from the word *vir,* "man," so literally means "manliness"—which to the Romans involved a combination of bravery, discipline, and self-sacrifice.

Virtus was first and foremost a military virtue. The Romans had always felt that military experience was essential for men in the upper classes. The leaders of the state had to have the ability to command, and the army was the best place to learn and practice this. Many reigning emperors made a point of giving their heirs a good taste of army life, as Trajan did with Hadrian. Not only did this help develop *virtus,* but it was the best way to earn the respect and loyalty of the legions. A man who had shared the hardships of camp life with the soldiers and led them to victory would sit all the more securely on his throne. And of course, army service in young

⁓ FOR THE FATHERLAND ⁓

One of the clearest expressions of what *virtus,* or "manliness," meant to upper-class Romans can be found in a poem from Horace's third book of Odes. The poem is untitled in Latin, but English translators sometimes call it "Discipline." Here are some selections from it:

Let the vigorous boy learn well to bear
Lean hardship like a friend in bitter war,
And let the fearsome man on horse
With his spear harass the fierce Parthian
　force. . . .*

Virtus, never knowing disgraceful defeat,
Shines with untarnished pride and respect
And neither takes up nor lays down its power
At the pleasure of the people's changing favor.

It is sweet and fitting to die for the fatherland.
Besides, death hunts down a fleeing man
And for unwarlike youth shows no mercy
To cowardly back or bended knees.

Virtus, opening heaven to the deserving,
Gives proper guidance past forbidden things
And rises on soaring wings above the crowds
Of the vulgar and the clinging ground.

* The Parthians, whose homeland was in what is now northeastern Iran, were among Rome's "archenemies."

manhood prepared the future emperor for his role as commander in chief.

Some emperors were more interested in military matters than others. Neither Gaius Caligula nor Nero ever led the army, and Claudius took no active military role in the invasion of Britain that he ordered. Vespasian became emperor because of his success as a general and his popularity with the troops, but after taking the throne he left active military command to his son Titus. Hadrian, on the other hand, was one of the emperors who was closely involved with the army both before and after coming to the throne. On a visit to Germany as emperor, Hadrian made a point of spending time among the legions stationed there. He improved their conditions and their discipline, largely through his own example, according to the *Augustan Histories:*

> Though more desirous of peace than of war, he kept the soldiers in training just as if war were imminent, inspired them by proofs of his own powers of endurance, actually led a soldier's life among [them] . . . , and, after the example of . . . his own adoptive father Trajan, cheerfully ate out of doors such camp-fare as bacon, cheese, and vinegar. . . . He incited others by the example of his own soldiery spirit; he would walk as much as twenty miles fully armed; he . . . generally wore the commonest clothing, would have no gold ornaments on his swordbelt or jewels on the clasp . . . , visited the sick soldiers in their quarters, selected the sites for camps, . . . banished luxuries on every hand, and, lastly, improved the soldiers' arms and equipment. . . . He made it a point to be acquainted with the soldiers and to know their numbers.

ᴠV᷂

IMPERIAL
WOMEN

THE EMPEROR REPEATEDLY ASSERTED THAT THERE MUST BE A LIMIT
TO THE HONORS PAID TO WOMEN.
—TACITUS, *ANNALS*

opposite:
**A portrait of a
Roman matron
seemingly lost
in thought**

The imperial court was very much a man's world. Of course the emperor's wife and children, and often his mother and sisters, lived with him in the palace. But these women and children, and their female slaves and freedwomen servants, were far outnumbered by the male members of the imperial household. In both the imperial family and senatorial families, women's activities were extremely limited. While men were out and about conducting legal business or serving in the government, women were expected to mostly stay close to home and concern themselves with household and family matters. Roman historians rarely wrote much about women; when they did, it was usually to criticize a woman for scandalous behavior—which might mean little more than getting

involved in too many activities outside the home. Roman women were praised for virtues such as bravery, strength, loyalty, and devotion to duty only when those virtues served the men in their families.

OLD-FASHIONED FAMILY VALUES

Roman society was set up to put all power in the hands of men. The male head of the family had absolute authority over all his children, and often over grandchildren and other relatives as well. He decided whom they married and could also order them to divorce for any reason he pleased. (Under Roman law, children remained with their father after a divorce.) He could disown family members and punish them harshly for misbehavior. All the family finances were controlled by him, and his consent was necessary for most major decisions made by other family members. This *patria potestas,* or "power of the father," was especially dominant in the lives of women, who could never become the heads of families.

The law generally required that a woman always have a male guardian, normally her father or husband, for her entire life. If he died, the courts would appoint another guardian. A woman could not handle financial, business, or legal matters without her guardian's permission and assistance. From the time of Augustus, however, the law allowed a freeborn mother of three children to be freed from guardianship.

The first emperor was very disturbed by recent trends in Roman society. People were often staying unmarried, or marrying later in life, or not having children when they did marry, especially in the upper class. Augustus wanted to change this situation, to strengthen the family and keep it at the center of society. He created laws that rewarded people for having three or more children, punished them (by reducing their right to inherit property) for remaining unmarried or childless, and required women to remarry after being widowed or divorced. These laws also tried to control other aspects of women's and men's private lives.

In spite of the legislation, the birthrate among the upper class does not seem to have increased. This was partly because pregnancy and childbirth were extremely risky for women in ancient times. Even with the best health care, many diseases and problems were not preventable, and there were few medical techniques that could help a woman if something went wrong during pregnancy or childbirth. Miscarriages were common and many women—and their babies—died from childbirth complications. Very often, parents who dearly wanted to have many children just were not able to. Among such parents was Augustus himself. His only child was his daughter, Julia, from his second marriage.

POWER BEHIND THE THRONE

Augustus divorced his second wife to marry Livia, who belonged to one of Rome's oldest and most influential noble families. She was already married and was pregnant with her second child, but the emperor ordered her husband to divorce her. After that, according to Suetonius, Livia was "the one woman he truly loved until his death." Augustus certainly valued her, trusting her to meet with ambassadors when he was busy with other matters. He not only asked her for advice on a regular basis but also took notes on what she said so that he could study it later. When Livia's son Tiberius succeeded to the throne, Livia expected her influence to continue. The new emperor, however, felt that his mother was

Livia and her son Tiberius as a child

A DAUGHTER RULED BY HER FATHER

Augustus was an old-fashioned father and insisted that his daughter, Julia, spend her time spinning and weaving like the virtuous Roman women of earlier days. (Julia and her stepmother made most of the emperor's clothes themselves.) She was strictly supervised, seldom allowed to go out, and was not allowed to have any boyfriends.

Like many upper-class Roman daughters, Julia was at the mercy of her father's ambitions. When she was fourteen, Augustus had her marry his nephew Marcellus, who was in his late teens at the time. The young man died two years later, in 23 B.C.E., leaving no children behind. Augustus was determined that Julia bear children who could succeed him, so in 21 B.C.E. he married her to his friend Agrippa—after making Agrippa divorce the wife he already had. Agrippa was twenty-five years older than Julia, but they had five children together, and Augustus adopted

A young woman picking spring flowers

the two oldest boys to be his heirs.

When Agrippa died in 12 B.C.E., the emperor worried about who would be his heirs' guardian if he should die, too. So Augustus forced his stepson Tiberius to divorce his much-loved wife and marry Julia. Tiberius never came to love—or even like—Julia, and life at court was unpleasant for him in other ways. With Augustus's permission, he left Rome and Julia (five years after their wedding) to live on the Greek island of Rhodes.

Julia took the opportunity to rebel against her strict upbringing and her arranged marriages. Roman authors later exaggerated her misconduct, but she certainly did not uphold her father's ideas about proper moral behavior for women. In 2 B.C.E., after denouncing her to the entire Senate, Augustus condemned Julia to exile. She died in despair sixteen years later, not long after her father's death.

were arranged, the spouses often grew to love and respect each other. Divorce was common and easy to obtain, and people often remarried after being widowed. But the ideal for both men and women was still felt to be lifelong marriage to one person. An upper-class husband, speaking at his wife's funeral in about 10 C.E., said, "Rare indeed are marriages of such long duration, which are ended by death, not divorce. We had the good fortune to spend forty-one years together with no unhappiness."

☙ A SENATOR'S WIFE ❧

Pliny the Younger, a senator with a successful law career and an excellent record in public service, was also a famous writer and orator. He was devoted to his young wife, Calpurnia, and praised her excellent qualities in this letter he wrote to her aunt:

My wife is very sensible and very thrifty. And she loves me, surely an indication of her virtue. She has even, because of her affection for me, taken an interest in literature. She has copies of my books, she reads them over and over again, and even learns them by heart. What anxiety she feels when I am going to plead a case in court, what great relief when I have finished! She even stations slaves to report to her on the approval and the applause I receive, and on what verdict I obtain in the case. And whenever I give a recitation, she sits nearby, concealed behind a curtain, and listens very eagerly to the praise I win. She even sets my poems to music and sings them, to the accompaniment of a lyre. No musician has taught her, but love itself, the best of instructors.

In this same eulogy, the husband praised his wife for excelling in traditional womanly qualities: "your modesty, obedience, affability, and good nature, your tireless attention to wool-working, your performance of religious duties without superstitious fear, your artless elegance and simplicity of dress . . . your affection toward your relatives, your sense of duty toward your family." This wife was so devoted to her husband that when she found she couldn't have children, she offered to let him divorce her so that he could try to have them with someone else. He answered, "How could the desire or need for having children be so great that I would break faith with you!"

As this eulogy indicates, household duties and, if possible, raising children were an upper-class woman's main responsibilities. A number of slaves and sometimes freedwomen helped her with these tasks. In addition, upper-class women had slaves to style their hair, take care of their clothes and cosmetics, and escort them through the streets. Roman women were able to go out to visit friends, go to the baths, attend banquets and birthday parties, take part in religious ceremonies (some for women only), and watch plays and public shows. At home a Roman lady might fill her leisure hours with reading, writing or dictating letters to friends, or playing a musical instrument.

A wealthy woman could benefit her family and community by using her inheritance to provide dowries for poor female relatives or funding the construction of a temple or other public building. One elderly lady who used some of her money for good causes such as these also used her wealth and leisure to indulge her love for popular entertainment. Although this behavior rather shocked the conservative writer Pliny the Younger, he praised her for mak-

With a slave standing by to wait on her, an upper-class woman entertains herself by playing the kithara, a harplike instrument from Greece.

ing sure that her pleasures didn't keep her grandson from developing proper Roman *gravitas:*

> Ummidia Quadratilla . . . owned a company of pantomime dancers and enjoyed their performances with more enthusiasm than was proper for a woman of her social rank. However, her grandson Quadratus, who was brought up in her household, never saw their performances, either in the theater or at home. . . . She herself told me . . . that she, during the idle hours which women have, used to relax by playing checkers or watching pantomimes; but when she was about to do either, she always told her grandson to go and study.

·VI·

CHILDREN OF THE EMPIRE

HE PASSED HIS BOYHOOD AND YOUTH IN THE CULTIVATION
OF EVERY WORTHY ATTAINMENT.
—TACITUS, *THE LIFE OF AGRICOLA*

All Roman babies were born at home. Fathers generally preferred sons to daughters, but wealthy families (who did not have to worry about having too many mouths to feed) were usually overjoyed by the birth of any healthy child. Nine days after birth, a ceremony of purification was held to protect the baby from evil. Then the child was formally named and given a *bulla,* a good luck charm often made of gold. Occasionally parents went even further to try to guarantee good fortune for their newborn. Gaius Caligula, for instance, carried his baby daughter Julia Drusilla to every temple of every goddess in Rome so that she would be blessed by them all.

Sometimes, even when a baby was born healthy, the mother did not survive childbirth. The father would then hire a wet nurse to

opposite:
A baby boy with his pet goose, carved in marble

56

breast-feed the baby. Some healthy Roman mothers felt that breast-feeding was beneath their dignity, and so their children, too, might be nurtured by wet nurses. Nurses were usually slaves or freedwomen. The first-century orator Quintilian recommended, "Above all, make sure that the infant's nurse speaks correctly. . . . Of course, she should without doubt be chosen on the basis of good moral character, but make sure that she speaks correctly as well. The child will hear his nurse first, and will learn to speak by imitating her words." A nurse often continued to care for a child after he or she was weaned, with lasting affection forming between the two.

One of a *paedagogus*'s duties was to protect his young charge—which included keeping the child out of fights like this one.

Another important person in a young child's life, especially a boy's, was the *paedagogus,* usually a slave. His job was to rock the cradle and babysit, then to play with the child, take him on outings, and teach him table manners and perhaps the beginnings of reading and writing. As a boy grew still older, the *paedagogus* became a protector who escorted him to and from school, the baths, the theater, and elsewhere, shielding him from any immoral influences on the way. Many boys grew up feeling the same affection for their *paedagogi* as for their nurses. As an expression of gratitude, these slaves often received their freedom when their charges became adults.

PLAYTIME AND SCHOOL DAYS

Upper-class Roman children had more time for play than poorer children, who often had to start helping their families at a very young age. And of course, being wealthy, children of imperial and senatorial families had their choice of many toys. Among others, there were dolls, balls, tops, marbles, board games, hobbyhorses, model chariots, and (though only for boys) wooden swords and shields. Some boys had miniature chariots that they could ride in, pulled by a goat.

☙ ROMAN CHECKERS ❧
A GAME TO PLAY TODAY

The Roman *ludus calculi,* or "game of stones," was popular with people of all ages. It's a little like checkers and is still fun today. The Romans played it with stones or glass markers, and their board was generally not checkered but just had a grid of lines marked on it. However, a regular checkerboard will work just fine. To start, each player needs thirty-five checkers. Or you can use small, smooth stones or some other kind of markers instead, so long as you have two different colors (in the instructions below, we'll assume they're black and red).

Black goes first. The players take turns placing their markers on the board, one at a time. There is no jumping or other movement of a marker once it's been placed. The goal is to be the first person to get five markers in a row. They can be in a horizontal, vertical, or diagonal line. The challenge is that you have to block the other player from completing his or her line at the same time you're working on yours.

Unless you have no other possible move, you are not allowed to make a "double open-ended three" in any direction, for example:

Otherwise you can place your markers in any way you like. If neither player gets five in a row and all the squares are filled, the game is a draw. Time to play again!

A boy reciting his lessons to his tutor. This image comes from the child's sarcophagus, or stone coffin; he died at the age of ten.

Roman children began learning from their parents at an early age. Parents were encouraged to make learning fun and not to push too hard. They usually taught the alphabet, the basics of reading, and perhaps some simple math. What was most important, though, was for the parents to give their children a moral education. They might do this by reading or telling stories about great Roman heroes of the past, so that children could learn from these famous examples of *gravitas, pietas,* and *virtus.*

Formal education typically began at about age seven. Children of very wealthy families were generally taught at home by tutors. Augustus hired a famous teacher to move into the palace and educate his grandsons. Many other emperors had palace schools where they employed the best tutors to instruct children of the imperial family. Children of favored senators and others might also be invited to the imperial school. Claudius, for instance, rewarded Vespasian for his military service in the invasion of Britain by giving his son Titus a court education.

The most important part of an upper-class boy's formal education was training in Latin and Greek, literature, and public speaking. Math was of next importance, but science was studied little, if at all. Many boys also studied philosophy, but the general opinion was that it was not proper for high-ranking Romans to be too interested in philosophy. As a boy, Hadrian was so fond of Greek literature and Greek philosophy that people nicknamed him Greekling. Hadrian didn't seem to mind, and continued to love all things Greek for the rest of his life. Many upper-class Roman boys, in fact, finished their formal education with a tour of Greece, where they could study with some of the best orators to be found.

Roman girls received much less education than boys. They did learn Latin and literature, perhaps Greek, and probably a little math. Training in public speaking was considered unnecessary, however; household skills were much more important. While the daughters of wealthy families would never need to cook or clean for themselves, they would have to supervise the slaves who did such work, and they usually were expected to know how to spin and weave.

BECOMING AN ADULT

Childhood ended very early for upper-class girls, who could (and often did) marry as young as twelve. Their husbands were usually in at least their midtwenties, but they might be quite a bit older, perhaps even in their fifties, having already been married once or twice. The marriage was often arranged for financial or political

❧ A TURBULENT CHILDHOOD ❧

Upper-class children grew up in a variety of settings and could experience huge ups and downs. As a young child, Gaius Caligula, along with his mother and siblings, lived in an army camp while his father was commanding the legions stationed in Germany. His parents often dressed him up in a miniature army uniform, including the tough sandals called *caligae*. Because of this the soldiers, who were fond of him, nicknamed him Caligula. Afterward he went with his parents to his father's next posting, in Syria, but there his father died (perhaps poisoned).

When Gaius was fifteen his second-oldest brother was arrested for treason. Two years later his mother and oldest brother were sent into exile because the emperor Tiberius suspected them of plotting against him. By the time Gaius was twenty-one, all three were dead. Meanwhile, he briefly lived with his grandmother, then was summoned to join the emperor on Capri, where he stayed until he himself became emperor.

reasons, and the girl's feelings might not be taken into account at all. It was her duty, and part of the virtue of *pietas,* to gladly accept her father's choice of a husband.

An older husband often took it on himself to finish his young wife's education, perhaps polishing her manners and her appreciation of literature. For example, Pliny the Younger had a friend who, he wrote, "has recently read me some letters which he said were written by his wife. . . . Whether they are really his wife's, as he says, or his own . . . one can only admire him either for what he writes, or the way he has cultivated and refined the taste of the girl he married."

Boys spent their teen years finishing their education, especially honing their public-speaking skills. Between the ages of fifteen and eighteen, it was time for the coming-of-age ceremony. An upper-class boy in Rome first went to the household shrine of his family's protector deities. There he left his *bulla* and his purple-bordered toga, the garment of childhood. This was replaced with the pure white toga of manhood. Then his family and friends accompanied him to the forum, where he was formally proclaimed a citizen. After a visit to the city's most important temple, the rest of the day was spent feasting and celebrating. Once a boy came of age, he could begin his career in the military and government.

VII
PRIVILEGE AND PERIL

I ADMIRE HIM ALL THE MORE FOR THIS VERY REASON, THAT AMID
UNUSUAL AND EXTRAORDINARY DIFFICULTIES HE BOTH
SURVIVED HIMSELF AND PRESERVED THE EMPIRE.
—DIO CASSIUS ON EMPEROR MARCUS AURELIUS

opposite:
This artist's reconstruction of part of a Roman villa shows the luxury and splendor that surrounded the patricians.

The senatorial families and the imperial court made up a small percentage of the people of ancient Rome. This minority controlled most of the empire's wealth. As we have seen, the patricians frequently used their wealth for the public good, from building temples and aqueducts to contributing funds to feed the poor. Like the rich and powerful of every time and place, they also spent their money on luxuries and entertainments. Those at the highest levels of power certainly enjoyed equally high privileges. At the same time, although they were secure from hunger and want, they were, like everyone else, vulnerable to illnesses and injuries. And when it came to struggles for power or the fears and whims of an unstable emperor, the patricians might pay a high price for living at the top of society.

THE BENEFITS OF GOOD LIVING

Wealthy Romans had perhaps the highest standard of living in the ancient world. They dressed in clothes of silk, linen, or the finest wool, often dyed in jewel-like colors. Women wore perfume, cosmetics, and plenty of jewelry; both sexes might dye their hair or wear wigs. Upper-class homes were spacious and beautifully decorated—and most well-off families had one or more country villas in addition to their house in Rome.

With all their needs attended to by slaves, Romans at this level of society had plenty of leisure time. Literary senators liked to hold and attend recitations, where poems, histories, and other works were recited, or read aloud, often by the author himself. Others enjoyed going to gladiator combats, wild-animal fights, and chariot races. Everyone liked to have a good afternoon bath and massage, perhaps with an exercise session or ball game first.

After bathtime came dinnertime, the highlight of many a Roman's day. Although Augustus was well known for preferring plain food such as bread, herring, cheese, and green figs, very few of his successors—or other wealthy Romans—were content with such simple meals. Banquets were held frequently, with numerous courses served on silver dishes. Along with good conversation, there was usually entertainment of some kind: plays, poetry readings, music, acrobats, or dancers. Sometimes banqueters enjoyed games or a little gambling. Writing of Augustus, Suetonius related that "at some dinner parties he would auction tickets for prizes of most unequal value, and paintings with their faces turned to the wall, for which every guest present was expected to bid blindly, taking his chance like the rest: he might either pick up most satisfactory bargains, or throw away his money."

⋙ EAT LIKE AN EMPEROR ⋘

Upper-class Romans often served elaborate dinners in their gardens. The guests reclined, leaning on their left elbows, on couches around a central table. People used knives for cutting meat and spoons for eating soup, but otherwise ate with their fingers. Dinnertime in ancient Rome came in late afternoon—and if dinner was a banquet, it could last for hours.

There were three parts to each dinner, and each could have many dishes. First came appetizers, then the main course, and finally dessert. Common appetizers were egg dishes, raw vegetables, and fish. The main course was meats and cooked vegetables. This was where the greatest variety and most elaborate preparation could come in. Dessert was generally fruit and pastries. The usual drink was wine, sometimes flavored with spices.

Emperors and wealthy Romans ate many exotic foods, such as sea urchins, roasted peacocks, and flamingoes' tongues. They had large staffs of well-trained slaves to cook and serve their meals. Today it would be difficult for most people to prepare a whole banquet fit for an emperor. But here is a version of a vegetable recipe that was created for the emperor Commodus:

INGREDIENTS:

- 1 lb. fresh green beans
- 1 tsp. ground pepper
- 1/2 tsp. ground celery seed
- a pinch of ground aniseed
- 2 tsp. chopped onions
- 1 cup chicken stock
- 3 well-beaten egg yolks

- Cook the beans in 1/2 cup water for just a few minutes. Drain the beans but save the water.
- For the sauce: in a bowl, mix together the pepper, celery seed, and aniseed. Add one tablespoon of the water the beans were cooked in. Stir in the onions, chicken stock, and egg yolks.
- Put the beans in a casserole. Pour the sauce over the beans.
- Bake at 325°F until the dish is firm.
- Serve and enjoy!

To entertain the common people, their courts, and themselves, emperors frequently produced spectacles, for example flooding an arena and staging mock sea battles. One of the most lavish productions of all was Gaius Caligula's two-mile-long bridge of boats. The emperor had merchant ships line up across the Bay of Naples, and a road was built on top of them. During two days of festivities Caligula, dressed in splendid costumes, raced across the boat-bridge, first on a fast horse and then in a two-horse chariot, accompanied by the entire Praetorian Guard and all his friends in chariots. Extravaganzas like this were impressive and enjoyed by many, but they were expensive to produce, even for an emperor. Too many spectacles of this sort would cause a drain on the imperial treasury—a sure sign of trouble coming.

DANGER IN HIGH PLACES

As we have seen, just because a man was emperor did not mean that he was indestructible. Half of the first twenty Roman emperors died from old age, strokes, or illnesses such as malaria and cancer. The other half died by violence. Two committed suicide, and the rest were assassinated. The murderers were nearly always people close to the emperor: Praetorian Guardsmen, freedmen of the court, even family members.

When it came to palace plots, women could be every bit the equal of men, it seems. Two of Gaius Caligula's sisters, for example, were involved in a conspiracy to overthrow him and were sent into exile. Claudius's third wife, Messalina, schemed to marry another man and make him emperor. (We have already encountered the plotting of Claudius's fourth wife, Agrippina.) There were many rumors about women at the imperial court who poisoned possible heirs so that their own sons or favorites could succeed to the throne.

The very possibility of conspiracies afflicted some emperors severely. Tiberius retired to the island of Capri largely because he was so worried about plots against him. Toward the end of his reign, his fears led to a large number of treason trials in Rome.

⬬ HOW TO SURVIVE LIFE'S TRIALS ⬬

The philosopher-emperor Marcus Aurelius was a follower of the Stoic school of philosophy. Stoicism taught that people should train themselves to be ruled by reason so that they would not be troubled by worries or strong emotions; this was the way to be truly happy and live in harmony with the universe.

Such beliefs probably served Marcus Aurelius well. During his reign, the empire's border along the Danube River was continually threatened by Germanic tribes. Marcus spent years at war along the Danube frontier, while at home an epidemic of the plague raged. It was during these troubled times that he began writing his *Meditations.* In the following passage, the emperor gives some guidelines for getting through the tough times:

The first rule is, to keep an untroubled spirit; for all things must bow to Nature's law, and soon enough you must vanish into nothingness, like Hadrian and Augustus. The second is to look things in the face and know them for what they are, remembering that it is your duty to be a good man. Do without flinching what man's nature demands; say what seems to you most just—though with courtesy, modesty, and sincerity.

Executions were sometimes carried out by throwing the offenders to wild animals in the amphitheater.

Nero, too, often suspected courtiers, senators, and even family members of conspiring to overthrow him. Like Tiberius, he was sometimes right. But Nero's drastic measures to deal with conspirators and potential troublemakers—executing or exiling many senators and others, sometimes on the slimmest evidence—made him even more likely to be the victim of plots.

Events like these show how dangerous it sometimes was to be part of the circle of power. The senator and author Pliny the Younger lived through the reign of Domitian, another emperor whose tyrannical behavior and extreme insecurity resulted in sweeping executions. Pliny experienced the last four years of Domitian's rule as "a time when seven of my friends had been put to death or banished . . . , and there were certain clear indications to make me suppose a like end was awaiting me." Tacitus, who also survived this period, described "the senate-house besieged," "the senate hemmed in by armed men," numbers of ex-consuls "falling at one single massacre," and "many of Rome's noblest ladies exiles and fugitives."

Today, Nero and Domitian are also remembered for relentlessly persecuting the early Christians. These persecutions and other acts of violence and cruelty are often the main things that many people associate with the Roman emperors. We need to balance this image, however, with the memory of those emperors who governed justly and well. Their world was not perfect, and yet it has left us much that is inspiring: great works of literature, structures that have stood for two thousand years, beautiful paintings and statues, and stories of bravery, love, and devotion among people much like us.

THE CITY

❦ I ❧

AN EMPIRE
OF CITIES

Even now, I see a city . . . greater than any other that is or
will be or was seen in ages past.
—Ovid, *Metamorphoses*

According to legend, Rome began with a
collection of shepherds, escaped slaves, and men
looking for a new start in life. Archaeologists have
recently proven that during the eighth century B.C.E.,
the early Romans—whoever they were—definitely
organized themselves and founded a city. Over the next few centuries, as history tells us, Rome expanded its rule to nearby cities
and the rural areas they controlled.

Many of Rome's neighbors had a similar culture and spoke the
same language, Latin, as the Romans. Other peoples of the area,
such as the Etruscans, were quite different. Rome conquered them
all, sometimes absorbing aspects of the conquered societies, but
always imposing its own language, laws, and government.

opposite:
**Many cities in
the Roman
Empire began
as military
bases, like the
one at which
these soldiers
are working.**

As Rome's territory grew, so did the variety of cultures it incorporated. Southern Italy had many Greek settlements; northern Italy was the home of Celtic tribes (related to the Welsh and Irish of today). Outside of Italy, the Romans took over numerous well-established cities in eastern and southern regions such as Greece, Syria, and Egypt. There were far fewer urban areas in northwestern Europe. Where the Romans did not find cities, however, they created them. The Roman Empire embraced many languages and cultures, but all of the provinces under Roman rule came to have at least one thing in common: the importance of cities.

THE NETWORK OF POWER

"Goddess of continents and peoples, O Rome, whom nothing can equal and nothing approach"—this was how the Spanish-born poet Martial addressed the city he had adopted as his home. His feelings were shared by many. Rome was the largest and most powerful city in the Western world. It was not only the capital of the empire, but was also a center of religion, literature, and culture. And it was home to more than a million people, a huge population for ancient times.

Rome reached its supreme status largely because of the great discipline, skill, and efficiency of the Roman army, for as the army won more territory, the city had more resources available to it. The Roman talent for organizing and engineering went hand in hand with this military might. When the soldiers of the Roman legions were not fighting, they were often at work on building projects, such as roads. These roads, in turn, made it easy for the legions, stationed throughout the empire, to receive supplies and deploy to trouble spots.

The impressive network of paved roads that connected the capital with the rest of the empire was not just for military use. Messengers traveled to and from the emperor with government communications. Students and tourists paid visits to the empire's great centers of learning and other famous sites. Merchants journeyed the roads with their carts and pack trains, loaded with olive oil, wine, cloth, produce, building materials, and other goods destined for the great city.

The Tiber River was another kind of roadway, linking Rome with the Mediterranean. From the port city of Ostia, barges made the twenty-mile trip upriver to Rome bearing a world of luxurious imports: silk and spices from the East, marble and works of art from Greece and Asia Minor, pearls and rare purple dye from Syria, linen and glass from Egypt. The most important cargo of all, however, was grain, shipped from Sicily and North Africa: more than six million sacks of grain a year were required to feed the people of the city of Rome.

A nineteenth-century artist's view of the Roman Forum, the city's center. In the foreground is the Arch of Septimius Severus; in the background, near the center, is the Colosseum.

THE CITY

Magnificent feats of Roman engineering, aqueducts were built all over the empire. This one can still be seen near Segovia, Spain.

A sure food supply was one of Rome's greatest needs. Equally important was the water supply. Roman engineering guaranteed that fresh water was plentiful—in the amount of some 250 million gallons a day. Eleven aqueducts brought this precious resource to the city from rivers and springs in the hills to the south and east. The water flowed in underground conduits or covered trenches for much of the way. To cross gorges and rivers, the conduits were laid over bridges supported by soaring arches. A water commissioner in 97 C.E. expressed the Romans' pride in these marvels of practical engineering in this way: "Will anybody compare the idle pyramids, or those other useless though renowned works of the Greeks with these aqueducts, these many indispensable structures?"

EXPORTING URBAN LIFE

Rome became the pattern for other cities in the empire. This was not so surprising in Italy, where generations of sharing a common culture naturally resulted in similar styles of building and urban development. Elsewhere, however, the Romans very deliberately promoted their own kind of urban lifestyle. For example, after southern Britain was conquered in the middle of the first century,

Roman governors encouraged the native people to abandon their scattered rural settlements. The historian Tacitus described how his father-in-law, Agricola, governor of Britain for a number of years, used "the charms of luxury" to persuade his subjects to stop fighting the Romans and embrace city-based Roman ways:

> Agricola gave private encouragement and public aid to the building of temples, courts of justice and dwelling-houses, praising the energetic, and reproving the indolent [lazy]. . . . He likewise provided a liberal education for the sons of the chiefs. . . . [T]hey who lately disdained the tongue of Rome now coveted its eloquence. Hence, too, a liking sprang up for our style of dress, and the "toga" became fashionable. Step by step they [the British people] were led to things which dispose to vice, the lounge, the bath, the elegant banquet. All this in their ignorance, they called civilization, when it was but a part of their servitude.

This reconstruction of a temple in second-century Britain shows a combination of native and Roman building styles.

Where the Romans didn't have to build new cities, they often renovated and expanded existing ones. Emperors or wealthy citizens financed the construction of Roman-style temples, public buildings, marketplaces, bathhouses, monuments, and theaters in the cities of Greece, Asia Minor, and North Africa. Roman benefactors also frequently improved water supplies (by building aqueducts), harbor facilities, and the like. Such actions earned the gratitude of the cities' leading citizens, who were happy to enjoy these benefits of Roman rule.

By the second century the Mediterranean world was dotted with "little Romes," cities whose architecture, language, money, and laws all expressed their belonging to the empire. A person from a city in Gaul (modern France and Belgium) could visit a city in what is now western Turkey, more than two thousand miles away overland, and feel almost perfectly at home. Everyone paid for things with the same selection of silver, brass, and bronze coins; nearly everyone spoke either Latin or Greek. The surroundings were familiar: here would be the city center with its markets, law courts, and statues of the emperors; here were the temples dedicated to the deities that were worshipped all over the Roman world; here was an aqueduct supplying bathhouses and fountains.

The Romans called this cultural, political, and economic unity *pax Romana*, usually translated as "the Roman peace." But in the ancient world, *pax* meant not only a state of harmony, but, more importantly, one of order, where everything worked according to "the rules"—that is, the Romans' rules.

THE ARMY'S ROLE

The Roman army played a major part in developing urban life throughout the empire. The army's first role in this process was of

~ CITIES GREAT AND SMALL ~

I used to think the city men call Rome
Was like our market-town, to which we come
On market days, and drive our kids to sell.
O foolishness.

The great Roman poet Virgil put those words into the mouth of a shepherd in northern Italy. It's no wonder that this country dweller was stupefied when he saw how much larger Rome was than the small town he visited on market day, for the imperial capital was home to more than a million people.

The next-largest cities in the empire were Alexandria (Egypt) and Carthage (in what is now Tunisia), each with a population of some 500,000. The Syrian cities of Antioch (now in Turkey) and Apamea had around 200,000 residents each. Ostia, twenty miles downriver from Rome, went from a modest coastal town to a city of 30,000 in the early second century, thanks to the ongoing development of Rome's port facilities there. Pompeii, in southern Italy, had a population of close to 20,000 before it was destroyed by a volcanic eruption in 79 C.E. Most Roman cities, however, especially in the provinces, were home to between 5,000 and 15,000 people. The market town of Virgil's shepherd may have had no more than a few thousand inhabitants.

course military, conquering new territory for Rome. Then, if a new province already had well-established cities, the Roman government used them as headquarters to administer the province. If there were no urban settlements in desirable locations, the Romans built their own. Every legion included the surveyors, architects, carpenters, and stonemasons—along with the manpower provided by the ordinary soldiers—needed for any construction project.

One example of an army-built city is Timgad, in what is now northern Algeria. The emperor Trajan ordered its construction, in 100 C.E., as a settlement for army veterans. These retired soldiers remained on reserve duty, and their town had a strategic location: its nearness to mountain passes allowed it to protect Roman-ruled territory from nomadic groups who lived to the south. The army

Some of the ruins of the North African city of Timgad, including a monumental arch constructed to honor the emperor Trajan

planned and constructed Timgad carefully, with streets laid out in an orderly grid pattern. The city boasted all the comforts of Rome, including fourteen bathhouses.

Even without planning, the Roman legions were responsible for founding numerous cities, many of which still exist today. When the army set up an encampment or built a fort, people from all over the region were attracted to the area. The soldiers, who needed supplies, made excellent customers for local goods and produce. Taverns and other businesses were established to serve the army bases. Many legionnaires formed relationships with local women and had children with them; after the men were discharged from the army, they frequently settled with their families near the camp or fort. As the population grew, a city developed, and as such cities spread through a province, Roman culture—and control—were assured.

II

PUBLIC PLACES AND PRIVATE SPACES

THE ROMAN PEOPLE EASILY FIND EXCELLENT PLACES
IN WHICH TO LIVE.
—VITRUVIUS, *THE TEN BOOKS ON ARCHITECTURE*

I magine you are going to visit a Roman city in Italy. The well-paved road you are traveling on leads you through fields and pastures, vineyards and olive groves. As you draw near to the city limits, the road is lined with impressive marble tombs belonging to the families of prominent citizens. The city itself may be walled, and you will have to enter it through an imposing gateway. Except in frontier provinces, city walls and fortified gates are now just symbolic of the empire's might, or they may have been left standing from more turbulent times. But these days, thanks to the *pax Romana,* there is no real need for a city to have such protections. Stay on the road, and it will take you right into the center of the city.

THE HUB OF ACTIVITY

From early times the heart of Rome had been its Forum. In the middle of the Forum was a large rectangular plaza where citizens could gather for political meetings, business discussions, celebrations, ceremonies, and socializing. Around this open area were important temples, the Senate House and other government buildings, and the basilica, a spacious meeting hall where courts of law were held. There were also buildings that housed shops, offices, and schoolrooms. From a platform called the Rostra, emperors and senators made speeches to the people; when a notable person died, a relative might deliver a funeral eulogy from the Rostra. Inscriptions and painted notices on the walls of Forum buildings informed

The forum of a Roman city was a mixture of temples, government buildings, monuments, statues, and open spaces.

citizens of new laws, court decisions, and other important news. The Forum was also the ideal place to erect statues and monuments to honor the emperors and other famous Romans of both past and present.

As Rome grew, the original Forum became too small and crowded to serve the city's population. By 117, five additional forums had been constructed nearby. The last, largest, and most splendid forum of all was built by the emperor Trajan, who paid for the whole thing from the riches of a recent conquest. The buildings in Trajan's Forum included two libraries (one for books in Latin, the other for books in Greek) and a grand basilica paved with marble floors and roofed with tiles of gilded bronze. Beside the Forum, Trajan had a marketplace constructed. An ancient version of a shopping mall, it housed around 150 shops, supplying the citizens of Rome with both luxuries and everyday needs.

Other cities in the empire had forums of their own. When the Romans took over a city or built a new city in conquered territory, constructing a forum was usually a priority. Forums were often expanded or renovated by emperors, sometimes as a gift when they were visiting a city. Prominent citizens also donated buildings and monuments to their city's forum. For example, one of the largest buildings in Pompeii's Forum was a headquarters for the local wool-processing industry, given to the city and the wool workers by a wealthy widow named Eumachia.

PLACES TO GO, PEOPLE TO MEET

Naturally, the forum was not the only place where a city's residents gathered. Just northeast of Rome's forums was the Campus Martius. This was described during the reign of Augustus by the Greek

geographer Strabo as "an admirably large field on which an enormous number of chariots and horses can race unimpeded and a host of people can daily play ball games and practise discus-throwing and wrestling." The Campus was also the site of temples, tombs, and other monumental structures, as well as of occasional military drills. Many other Roman cities had similar athletic fields.

Nearly every urban neighborhood had a public well or fountain, near which people often lingered for a chat. Marketplaces were good locations for socializing as well as shopping. As in a modern city, friends or business associates frequently met up on the sidewalk; in some Roman cities the sidewalks were shaded by roofs supported by columns. There were taverns, food stands, and cookshops, too.

A nineteenth-century artist imagined this Roman street scene, complete with musicians and a performing monkey to entertain passersby.

❧ A ROMAN BATH ❧

Bathing was an important part of a Roman's daily routine. Women usually bathed in the morning, while men bathed in the afternoon, before dinner. The very wealthy had bathing facilities in their homes, but most city dwellers went to a public bathhouse. The baths were open to everyone who could pay the small entrance fee, and sometimes admission was free, paid for by the emperor or some other dignitary.

A full Roman bath was an elaborate affair. Bathers undressed in a changing room that contained compartments for storing clothes. Then they went into a *sudatorium*, which was like a sauna or steam bath. After working up a sweat, they entered a room called the *caldarium*. Here they sprinkled themselves with hot water from a large tub and used a metal scraper to remove dirt and perspiration. (These hot rooms were heated by an underfloor furnace system called a hypocaust.) Next came the *tepidarium*, a warm room where bathers could begin to cool off. Then it was time to move on to the *frigidarium* for a plunge into a cold pool. The last stop was the *unctorium*, where they could be massaged and rubbed with oil.

Large bathhouses had facilities for exercising and socializing as well as for washing. Many had gymnasiums, exercise grounds, ball courts, and swimming pools. There might also be sculpture galleries, gardens, libraries, reading rooms, and rooms for gaming and conversation. Vendors and snack bars sold food and drinks to bathers. For the Romans, a bath was as much a form of recreation as a way to get clean.

Though it is now in ruins, this twelve-seater restroom was once part of a public bathhouse in a North African city.

Public bathhouses were among the favorite places for people to meet, whether to socialize or talk business. At one point there were more than eight hundred bathhouses in Rome alone. Many of them were huge, splendid buildings, decorated with colored marble and works of art. Public lavatories (which charged an entrance fee) were also favorite gathering places, for the Romans were experts at making a virtue of a necessity. A public restroom in an ancient Roman city usually had about twenty seats arranged in a semicircle or open rectangle. The seats were often of marble, and behind them niches held statues of heroes, gods, and goddesses. Channels of constantly running water flowed under the seats to carry away sewage. In the middle of the bathroom there might be a fountain, and sometimes the room was heated by a furnace under the floor. For urban Romans, it seemed perfectly natural to sit down to a friendly conversation in these surroundings.

ISLANDS FOR THE MASSES

The majority of Roman city dwellers probably spent as little time as possible in their homes, which tended to be small, dark, cold in the winter, and hot in the summer. There was rarely indoor plumbing—the great water supply brought in by the aqueducts was mainly for public use in fountains, bathhouses, and lavatories. Artificial light was typically supplied by pottery lamps that burned olive oil, although candles might be used in provinces that didn't grow olives. The fireplace had not been invented yet; the usual heat source was a brazier, a kind of pan full of smoldering charcoal, supported by a tripod or other stand. Cooking was generally limited to whatever could be warmed by the brazier.

Such were the conditions in Roman apartment houses, which were called *insulae,* literally "islands." Like islands, these buildings rose up out of the urban "sea," three to five stories tall. A typical *insula* might house between thirty and fifty people. Some buildings had spacious apartments, with windows of mica, clear gypsum, or glass. There might be a central courtyard with a cistern, or tank, to hold water for the tenants' use. The remains of buildings like these are still standing in Ostia, and they are solidly constructed of concrete faced with brick. But a great many *insulae* were slums, shabbily constructed, with cramped apartments and nothing to cover the window openings except wooden shutters or oiled paper. The poet Juvenal wrote of such apartment buildings in Rome: "We inhabit a city propped up for the most part by slats: for that is how the landlord patches up the crack in the old wall, bidding the inmates sleep at ease under the ruin that hangs above their heads."

In more "upscale" *insulae,* the ground floor was often like a private house, occupied by the building's owner or rented by a single family. More commonly, the ground floor of an *insula* was devoted to stores or workshops, which were sometimes little more than booths opening to the street. In either case, this was the only floor that might have a lavatory; people in the upper stories had to make

do with chamber pots, which they were supposed to empty into a vat under the stairs. Sometimes, however, people just dumped the contents of their chamber pots out the window; if they hit a passerby, however, they could be hauled into court and fined.

A model of a street in the port city of Ostia. On the right is a well-built *insula*; at left, a grand single-family home.

A HOUSE IN TOWN

There were more than 46,000 *insulae* in the city of Rome, but only about 1,800 single-family houses—homes of the wealthy and privileged. Even in some of these, rooms on either side of the entryway were used as shops, often run or rented by slaves or freedmen of the family. (The shops were usually walled off from the rest of the building.) Otherwise the only opening on the front of the house was the door—for security and privacy, there were no windows looking out on the street.

The town houses of the wealthy, at least in Italy, generally followed a similar design. The entrance hall led into a large room called an atrium, which was used as a living room and a place to receive guests. Part of the atrium was unroofed, and beneath this opening was a rectangular pool to catch rainwater. Bedrooms and

ᵔᵔ A HOUSE FOR EVERY LIFESTYLE ᶜᵔ

One of the treasures of Roman literature is *The Ten Books on Architecture* by Vitruvius, probably written sometime during the reign of Rome's first emperor, Augustus (died 14 C.E.). Vitruvius dedicated this work to the emperor,

> because I saw that you have built and are now building extensively, and that in future also you will take care that our public and private buildings shall be worthy to go down to posterity by the side of your other splendid achievements. I have drawn up definite rules to enable you, by observing them, to have personal knowledge of the quality both of existing buildings and those which are yet to be constructed. For in the following books I have disclosed all the principles of the art [of architecture].

Vitruvius set out to write a complete description of his chosen art, covering such topics as the education of an architect, the properties of different kinds of timber and stone for building, the best place to establish a city and its public buildings, and the proper proportions and designs for temples to various gods and goddesses. The sixth book deals

with private houses. In the following excerpt, Vitruvius describes how houses should be planned "to suit different classes of persons":

Men of everyday fortune do not need entrance courts, tablina, or atriums built in grand style, because such men are more apt to discharge their social obligations by going round to others than to have others come to them.

Those who do business in country produce must have stalls and shops in their entrance courts, with crypts, granaries, storerooms, and so forth in their houses, constructed more for the purpose of keeping the produce in good condition than for ornamental beauty.

For capitalists and farmers of the revenue [businessmen who bid on government contracts, including tax collectors], somewhat comfortable and showy apartments must be constructed, secure against robbery; for advocates [lawyers] and public speakers, handsomer and more roomy, to accommodate meetings; for men of rank who, from holding offices and magistracies, have social obligations to their fellow-citizens, lofty entrance courts in regal style, and most spacious atriums and peristyles, with plantations [gardens] and walks of some extent in them, appropriate to their dignity. They need also libraries, picture galleries, and basilicas, finished in a style similar to that of great public buildings, since public councils as well as private law suits and hearings before arbitrators are very often held in the houses of such men.

A Roman bedroom decorated with beautifully frescoed walls. The mosaic floor combines geometric designs with a scene from mythology.

sitting rooms opened off the atrium. Toward the back, on either side, were recesses that housed small statues or paintings of the family's ancestors and protector gods. Behind the atrium was the *tablinum,* where the head of the family had his office. Next to the *tablinum* was a common location for the dining room. At the back of the house there was usually a peristyle, a courtyard or garden area surrounded by a covered walkway. Rooms opening off the peristyle might include the kitchen, slave quarters, storerooms, and sometimes a bath, a lavatory, and a stable. Really large and luxurious houses had even more rooms. For example, one lavish house in Pompeii had two atriums and two peristyles. There could also be an additional dining room, an extra room for entertaining, a picture gallery, a library, and elaborate gardens.

A family's wealth and culture were expressed by the way the

house was decorated, with mosaic floors, frescoed walls, and elegant fountains and sculptures in the peristyle or garden. Mosaics were often done in abstract designs or geometric patterns, but sometimes they made elaborate pictures or spelled out messages (such as *Cave canem,* "Beware of the dog," found in

A wordless "Beware of the dog" mosaic from the entryway to a Roman home

many entryways). Frescoes could also be abstract, but often they showed landscapes or scenes from mythology. Dining rooms frequently had frescoes or mosaics depicting fruit, shellfish, or other types of food. This was an example of the Roman devotion to propriety, one of the most important elements of architecture according to the architect Vitruvius, who called propriety "that perfection of style which comes when a work is authoritatively constructed on approved principles."

·III·

WORKING FOR A LIVING

HELLO PROFIT!

—MOSAIC FLOOR FROM POMPEII

ith no really effective artificial light sources, the Romans depended almost completely on natural light. To take the best advantage of daylight, they were usually up by sunrise. Breakfast was a quick meal of bread and perhaps cheese, washed down with water. Then it was off to work. Many shopkeepers and craftsmen lived in lofts above their stores or workshops, or in rooms behind them. Other workers would have to head through the crowded streets to their jobs.

Main streets in Roman cities were generally paved with stone and had raised sidewalks on either side. There were pedestrian crossings with stepping-stones that led from sidewalk to sidewalk. The stepping-stones helped protect people from mud and animal

opposite:
A food vendor sells round loaves of bread from his stall in a public square in Pompeii.

Stepping-stones, like these in Pompeii, helped people get from one sidewalk to another with relatively clean, dry feet.

droppings in the street. Most people traveled about the city on foot. The wealthy, however, might ride in litters or chairs carried by slaves. Wheeled traffic was banned between sunrise and dusk, with the exception of dignitaries' chariots on specific special occasions and wagons hauling materials for building projects. So those who made their living by carting goods into the city were forced to do their work in the dark of night.

SLAVE LABOR

Slavery was a fact of life in the Roman Empire, as it was throughout the ancient world. It was very common to take huge numbers of captives from a country defeated in war, and for some time Rome's conquests supplied the empire with most of its slaves. After the empire's borders became more settled, the majority of slaves were people born into slavery, for the children of slaves were also slaves.

Historians estimate that slaves made up about 30 percent of Rome's population. The city itself owned a number of slaves, who

did administrative work, maintained the aqueducts, cleaned and repaired streets and public buildings, and worked on construction projects. Some wealthy Romans owned hundreds of slaves, and even people with modest incomes might have one or two. Some slaves worked in or even ran businesses for their masters; others were rented out to people who only needed a slave for a short time. Still other slaves were entertainers of one kind or another: gladiators, chariot racers, actors, singers, dancers, and acrobats. A large number of urban slaves worked in their owners' households as secretaries, accountants, librarians, doctors, midwives, wet nurses, teachers, hairdressers, barbers, maids, masseurs, cooks, launderers, housecleaners, doorkeepers, litter carriers, torchbearers, and so on.

Barbarians defeated in war, like the man on the ground here, often became slaves consigned to do heavy manual labor.

The Roman economy was greatly dependent on slave labor. Keeping slaves from rebelling, therefore, was always a concern. Until the second half of the first century, slaves had no legal standing or protection, and owners could treat them however they wanted. Some masters used violence or the fear of violence to keep slaves obedient. We read of a cook being beaten for burning a meal, of a lady's maid having her hair pulled and her clothing torn for not curling her mistress's hair properly.

In 61 C.E. a mistreated slave killed his master, a high-ranking city official in Rome. The victim's friends wanted all four hundred of his slaves put to death, to discourage other slaves who might think of murdering their owners. Many Romans protested against this cruel punishment. The Senate debated the matter and finally decided to allow the mass execution. As one senator put it, "You cannot control these dregs of society except through fear."

Other Romans, however, felt that it was better to treat slaves with some kindness and respect. Well-treated slaves who had the hope of eventually gaining their freedom were more likely to accept their state of servitude. Besides, some Romans argued, to treat slaves decently was simply the right and humane thing to do. This idea was expressed by the playwright-philosopher-statesman Seneca the Younger when he wrote to a friend,

> I was happy to learn from people who had just visited you that you live on friendly terms with your slaves. . . . Some people say, "They're just slaves." But they are our fellow human beings! "They're just slaves." But they live with us! "They're just slaves." In fact, they are our fellow slaves, if you stop to consider that fate has as much control over us as it has over them. . . . I don't want to engage in a lengthy discussion of the treatment of slaves, toward whom we are very arrogant, very cruel, and very abusive. However, this is the essence of my advice: "Treat those of lower social rank as you would wish to be treated by those of higher social rank."

Household slaves were generally more fortunate than other slaves. Many were given an education or training in skilled crafts. Slaves who worked closely with their owners often had the opportunity to get to know them well, and a kind of friendship could grow between master and slave. Such slaves might receive gifts of money from their masters and even from their masters' friends; slaves were frequently able to save up enough to buy their freedom.

Pressing grapes into wine was only one of the tasks assigned to slaves who worked on country estates.

Owners sometimes freed slaves out of gratitude for their service; it was very common for people to write a will that freed many or all of their slaves. There were even cases of childless couples freeing then adopting a favorite slave.

Freedmen and freedwomen often continued doing the same jobs they had performed as slaves. They still had to show loyalty and work a certain number of days a year for their former owners. But freed slaves became Roman citizens, with voting rights for the men. The children of freedpersons were completely free and, if they were wealthy enough, could even run for public office and rise to the top ranks of Roman society. However, few attained this level of success.

GOODS AND SERVICES

In a Roman city, a large number of jobs could be done by slaves, freedpersons, or freeborn people of the lower class. Regardless of their status as free or slave, workers in the same craft or trade

Cushion makers in Rome show their wares to prospective customers.

banded together in some cities to form what we might call guilds. These associations hosted dinners for their members and often paid members' funeral expenses. Like modern trade unions, the guilds also endorsed political candidates. Graffiti from walls in the southern Italian city of Pompeii campaigned to passersby with slogans such as, "The muleteers urge the election of Gaius Julius Polybius."

The goods produced in Roman cities might be used locally or shipped to other parts of the empire. Many Romans were skilled artisans, among them leatherworkers, woodworkers, stoneworkers, and metalworkers. Some produced luxury items such as dyes, cosmetics, perfumes, jewelry, mosaics, furniture, wall paintings, and garden ornaments. Numerous shops were small individual or family businesses, where the artisan both made and sold goods in the same place. There were also large workshops or factories employing many people, which produced a variety of foodstuffs and manufactured goods, for example fish sauce, olive oil, wine, pottery, lamps, bricks, glassware, and cloth. Providing food and drink kept numerous city workers busy, including bakers, butchers, fishmongers, chicken sellers, innkeepers, and snack-bar operators. Then there were auctioneers, town criers, carters, porters, water carriers, boatmen, bathhouse attendants, sewer cleaners, construction workers, veterinarians—the list of occupations could go on and on. In addition, in many urban areas some people went out every day to work on farms outside the city limits.

A baker tends his oven.

Even with so many jobs to do, however, there were people who couldn't get work, especially in Rome. Some worked as day laborers or did odd jobs. Even some workers with full-time employment could not earn enough to support their families. Urban rents were very high, and so were other prices. For example, a pound of chicken could cost a tailor a full day's wages; a pair of boots for a mule driver cost him nearly five days' earnings. Freeborn workers had no health care plans, unemployment insurance, or other job benefits. For all of these reasons, free Romans sometimes had a much harder time than many slaves whose masters provided them with food, clothing, housing, and medical care.

PREJUDICE AGAINST FOREIGNERS
AND FREEDMEN

Many of Rome's workers were freedpersons or immigrants from Greek-speaking cities in the East. Some Romans resented these people contributing "foreign ideas" to society and "taking jobs away" from free citizens. The satirists Martial and Juvenal both expressed this prejudice, sometimes in an exaggerated manner. "Grammarian, orator, geometer, painter, wrestling-master, prophet, tightrope walker, medical man, wizard—he can do anything, your penniless Greek," Juvenal commented sarcastically. Martial complained:

Fortune, do you really think this situation is fair? Maevius, who was not born in Syria or Parthia or bought at a Cappadocian slave auction, but who was native-born, . . . a citizen who is pleasant, honest, a blameless friend, who knows both Latin and Greek . . . shivers in a cheap gray garment, while Incitatus, a freedman, a former mule driver, shines forth in scarlet.

The satiric novelist Petronius made one of his characters, a freedman, answer these kinds of objections with the following indignant speech to a dinner guest who had been making fun of him.

I hope that I now conduct my life so that no one can laugh at me. I'm a man among men; I hold up my head when I walk; I don't owe anyone a cent. . . . I bought myself a bit of land and saved up some cash. I feed twenty bellies and a dog.* I bought freedom for the slave woman who had shared my bed.** . . . For my own freedom I paid 1000 silver coins. . . . I was a slave for forty years. . . . I arrived in this town when I was a young boy. . . . I worked hard, and pleased my master. . . . I made my way successfully—and that's real success! Being born a free man is as easy as saying "Boo." So what are you staring at now, you stupid, smelly goat?

*In other words, he is now well-off enough to maintain his own household, including a number of slaves.
**Slave marriages were not legal, but slave couples still formed lasting relationships.

⸙IV⸙

ROMAN MEN:
FROM HIGH TO LOW

IF YOU ASK SOMEONE, "WHAT DID YOU DO TODAY?" HE WILL
ANSWER, "I WENT TO A COMING-OF-AGE PARTY; I ATTENDED AN
ENGAGEMENT PARTY AND THEN A WEDDING; ONE MAN ASKED ME TO
BE A WITNESS AT THE SIGNING OF HIS WILL, ANOTHER ASKED ME FOR
LEGAL ADVICE, A THIRD ASKED ME TO SIT IN COURT."
—PLINY THE YOUNGER, *LETTERS*

ather knows best" could have been ancient
Rome's motto. The Romans called their country
patria, "the fatherland." This is the root of our word "patriotic," and comes from the Latin word for "father," *pater*.
For the Romans, father and country were inseparable.
Their whole society revolved around their ideas of the duties and
privileges of fathers. The *pater familias*, "father of a family," was the
head of the household, with absolute authority over every member
of his family. He was responsible for their support and welfare, and
also exercised whatever discipline was necessary to make sure that
they behaved as proper members of society. It was his right to decide
even who they married (or divorced) and what they did for a living.
The Roman state worked in a similar way. Members of the upper class, who

opposite:
A group of
senators, men
at the highest
level of Roman
society

controlled virtually everything, were called *patricii* (patricians), "those with fatherly qualities." One of the highest honors a Roman man could receive was to be named *pater patriae*, "father of the fatherland," and Roman emperors were often given this title. The state was thought of as a very large extended family, which the emperor was supposed to oversee like a stern but caring father.

PATRONS AND CLIENTS

Another word related to *pater* was *patronus*, "defender." In ancient Rome a *patronus*, or patron, was a man whom a number of other men depended on to look out for their interests, advise them, help them in times of trouble, give them gifts, and so on. These were the patron's clients. They in turn owed the patron loyalty and various services, such as accompanying him to the forum when he had important business there or campaigning and voting for him in local elections. The more clients a man had, the more influence he had, and the higher his status was. One of the reasons that the emperor Augustus was able to rise to power was that he had a huge number of clients, probably more than any other man in Rome.

Freed slaves became their former masters' clients. Freeborn men also had patrons, and even a patron with a number of clients would have a patron of his own, a man of higher rank. Patronage was a kind of ladder, where every man was a client of someone on the rung above him. At the top of the ladder was the emperor. He alone had no patron, except perhaps Jupiter, the chief god of the Roman state.

Almost the first thing a Roman man did after getting up was go to wish his patron good morning. This visit was a show of respect, and the patron might have some errand or task he wanted a client

GREEDY CLIENTS AND RUDE PATRONS

The patron-client relationship had been an important part of Roman life for hundreds of years. By the middle of the first century, however, many a client seemed to have little real respect for his patron. As Seneca the Younger expressed the situation in one of his letters, "Once upon a time, clients sought a politically powerful friend; now they seek loot." The poet Martial wrote about what happened when he forgot to use the title *dominus*, "lord," when speaking to his patron: "This morning I address[ed] you, as it chanced, by your own name, nor did I add 'My Lord.' . . . Do you ask how much such casual conduct has cost me? It has robbed me of a hundred farthings." That was the risk a client took for offending his patron—the client might not receive his usual handout, money that he sometimes depended on to buy food or pay his rent.

Patrons could also behave disrespectfully. In one of his essays, Seneca the Younger complained about haughty patrons who acted as though it was an annoying chore to receive their clients' morning greetings:

How many patrons are there who drive away their clients by staying in bed when they call, or ignoring their presence, or being rude? How many are there who rush off on a pretense of urgent business after keeping the poor client waiting for a long time? How many avoid going through an atrium packed with clients and escape through a secret back door, as if it were not ruder to avoid a client than to turn him away? How many . . . will yawn disdainfully at men who have interrupted their own sleep in order to wait upon his [the patron's] awakening, and will mumble a greeting through half-open lips, and will need to be reminded a thousand times of the client's name?

to do. The client generally hoped to receive a gift or handout, or perhaps a dinner invitation. Most patrons invited their clients to dinner now and then, and often this was the only time a poor man had a really good meal. A stingy or arrogant patron, however, might serve his clients inferior food and drink, while higher-ranking guests at the same dinner joined the host in a meal of the best quality.

UPPER-CLASS TASKS

Men with the rank of senator were at the top of Roman society. They did not have to work for a living; in fact, it was actually illegal for them to earn money through their own labor. Senators were the great landowners of the empire, and most of their income came from the sale of the produce on their farming estates. With agents acting for them, members of the senatorial class also profited from property rentals, business investments, and moneylending.

Because senators were the wealthiest of Roman citizens, they were expected to devote themselves to government service. And only the rich *could* afford to serve in the government: not only were officeholders unpaid, but they were expected to spend a great deal of their own money on public works, entertainments, and gifts to the common people. Even when they served as lawyers, they worked for free.

One of the most important senators in Rome was the city prefect, who was appointed by the emperor. Responsible for maintaining law and order, he commanded the urban cohort, as many as 4,500 soldiers who formed a kind of police force. The city prefect also inspected markets to make sure meat prices were fair, and he had the power to prohibit individuals from engaging in business, professional, or legal activities.

⚜ DRESSING FOR SUCCESS ⚜

Nothing says "Roman" like the toga, the garment that clothed male citizens for centuries. The toga was an oblong of heavy white woolen cloth, roughly eighteen feet in length. It was worn over a tunic of linen or wool that reached to the knees. A man wrapped the toga around himself (usually with some assistance) in complicated drapes and folds. One part of the cloth hung from the left shoulder to the right thigh in a way that formed a pocket. Another part of the toga draped so that it could be pulled up over the head as a hood, which was necessary for religious ceremonies.

The toga was difficult to put on and often cumbersome to wear. Another problem was that it was supposed to be kept sparkling white, which meant that it frequently had to be sent to the cleaners for a good scrubbing. This made it wear out rather quickly—fortunately, patrons traditionally gave each client a new toga every year. This was a good thing, since clients were expected to wear the toga when making the morning visit to their patrons.

Many men took off their togas whenever they could, preferring the simple comfort of their tunics. A light, full-skirted kind of tunic called a *synthesis* became the preferred wear for dinner parties. (Fashion-conscious men might change into a different *synthesis* for each course of the meal.) Eventually, so many men were running around without their togas that several emperors passed laws to make sure that Rome's male citizens dressed with proper dignity. During the second century the emperor Hadrian, for example, ordered senators and equestrians "to wear the toga whenever they appeared in public except when they were returning from a banquet."

Below the senators ranked the equestrians. To belong to this class, a man did not have to be as wealthy as a senator, but he was still far richer than the majority of people in the empire. Equestrians were typically involved in "big business," making money as importers and exporters, shipowners, bankers, bidders on government contracts, and the like. Some military and government positions were open to equestrians, and these opportunities increased as the empire went on.

While Rome's government was in the hands of the emperor and his appointees, in many other cities of the empire men of the upper classes could run for election to town offices. The graffiti from Pompeii show that local political life could be quite lively. Elections were held every year to choose two *duovirs,* or co-mayors, and an aedile, who supervised the markets, public buildings, and public works. Often there was also some kind of town council, made up of wealthy freeborn men.

ARMY LIFE

Soldiers were a familiar sight in Roman cities—but not always a welcome sight. In camp soldiers lived according to strict discipline, but when they were out on the town they had a reputation for bullying civilians. Since a soldier could only be disciplined by his commander, a civilian filing a complaint had little hope of justice, as Juvenal pointed out in one of his *Satires:* "Your teeth are shattered? Face hectically inflamed, with great black welts? You know the doctor wasn't too optimistic about the eye that was left. But it's not a bit of good your running to the courts about it. If you've been beaten up by a soldier, better keep it to yourself."

For some 125,000 to 165,000 men, the army was their career for

most of their lives. The requirements for joining the Roman legions were strict. Recruits had to be Roman citizens*, and they had to meet high standards of physical fitness. They had to be mentally tough, too, with a strong team spirit, and for good reason: When the army was on campaign, the soldiers lived in leather tents, eight men to a tent. On the march, each group of eight shared a mule, which carried the tent and some supplies. The men themselves carried not only their weapons but also the necessary equipment for any construction projects they might have to undertake. The first-century historian Josephus described a Roman legion on the march this way:

> Then they march forward, everyone silent and in correct order, each man maintaining his particular position in the

Roman soldiers, including (far right) a *cornicen*, or military horn player. The Roman army used horns and trumpets to signal various commands to the troops.

*All freeborn Italians were citizens. Freeborn people in the provinces became citizens as a reward for service to the empire. Freed slaves, whether in Italy or the provinces, automatically received citizenship along with their freedom. The children of citizens also held Roman citizenship. Only citizens enjoyed the full protection of the law.

ranks, just as he would in battle. The infantry are equipped with breastplates and helmets, and carry a sword on both sides. . . . The infantry chosen to guard the general carry a spear and a small round shield. The rest of the soldiers carry a javelin and an oblong shield. However, they also carry a saw, a basket, a shovel, and an ax, as well as a leather strap, a scythe, a chain, and three days' food rations. As a result, an infantryman differs little from a loaded pack mule.

Serving in the Roman legions was far more of a commitment than enlisting in a modern army. Once a man joined up, he was required to stay for twenty-five years. If he deserted and was caught, he was executed. Discipline was harsh, and training was rigorous.

Roman foot soldiers, armed with spears and shields, accompanied by mounted troops who functioned mainly as scouts and messengers

The cost of a soldier's armor, equipment, and food was deducted from his pay. Legions were generally stationed near the empire's frontiers, or in trouble spots far from Italy. Moreover, until 197 C.E. legionary soldiers were not allowed to marry (although they frequently had long-term, but unofficial, relationships with women who lived near the army bases).

The army offered some opportunities for promotion. An ambitious man might rise to the rank of centurion, a commander who earned as much as sixty times the pay of ordinary legionnaires. Retired centurions often became important, respected men in their communities. Every soldier who survived his twenty-five years of service received a retirement bonus that equalled close to fourteen years' pay. The hope of such rewards was enough to make the army an appealing career choice for many men, especially those who had few other opportunities. The historian Tacitus, a senator during the first century, remarked on this fact a little scornfully: "It is chiefly the needy and the homeless who adopt by their own choice a soldier's life."

·V·

CITY WOMEN

GUARDIANS ARE APPOINTED . . . FOR FEMALES BOTH BEFORE AND
AFTER PUBERTY BECAUSE THEY ARE THE WEAKER SEX AND ARE
IGNORANT IN BUSINESS AND LEGAL MATTERS.
—ULPIAN, *RULES*

In many ways, the Roman Empire was a man's world. Women had far fewer rights and opportunities than they have in most industrialized nations today. Even women who were full Roman citizens could not vote or hold office. Women had to have male guardians to handle their legal and financial affairs.* However, women could inherit money and property and often were able to control it themselves thanks to loopholes in the law. We know that many wealthy city women used some of their money to benefit their communities by funding building projects and charities. Unfortunately, we do not know as much about ancient Roman women as we would like to, since nearly all the surviving writings are from men's points of view—and few male authors were interested in writing about women's lives.

opposite:
This richly colored fresco portrays a woman of Pompeii.

*Freeborn women could be released from guardianship after having three children; freedwomen earned the same privilege after bearing four children. Guardianship rules gradually loosened: by the middle of the second century, a woman could make out her own will without her guardian's advice or approval.

A well-to-do young woman who enjoys the finer things: her hair is fashionably dyed blond, her bracelets are gold, and she is refilling a flask of perfume.

WEALTHY WIVES

The amount—and kind—of freedom a woman enjoyed depended largely on her wealth and social class. An upper-class woman had many slaves to help her in the home, so she was able to go out to visit friends, exercise and relax at the baths, or attend public shows. She could also spend her leisure time reading, playing board games, or playing a musical instrument. A few upper-class women wrote poetry or other works, though little of these survive. Many Roman men, however, were offended if women showed too much intelligence, as Juvenal expressed in his *Satires:* "Don't marry a woman who speaks like an orator—or knows every history book. There should be some things in books which she doesn't understand. I hate a woman who . . . always obeys all the laws and rules of correct speech, who quotes verses I've never even heard of."

The ideal for Roman women, especially of the upper classes, was often portrayed in funeral eulogies such as this one for a woman named Murdia: "My dearest mother won the greatest praise of all, because she was like other good women in her modesty, decency, chastity, obedience, wool-work, zeal and loyalty." These were the qualities that Roman men valued most in wives, mothers, and daughters. Wool working, by the way, was traditionally women's main work: spinning thread, weaving cloth, and sewing the family's clothes. In the early empire, many upper-class women still did these things themselves; later, they usually only oversaw the wool working of their household slaves.

An upper-class Roman woman's main duty was to bear and raise children. This was, in fact, a dangerous job. Even with the best doctor or midwife, there was a lot that could go wrong during pregnancy and childbirth, and a large number of mothers and babies died. Miscarriages were also common. Many women had trouble getting pregnant in the first place. For all of these reasons, most upper-class women had only one to three children, even though large families were the ideal.

WORKING-CLASS WOMEN

While women of the upper classes enjoyed freedom from hard work, they had little control over their personal lives. Their marriages were always arranged, frequently for the sake of financial or political advantages for their fathers. For the same reasons, fathers could (and did) order daughters to divorce and then marry men with better connections. Divorce was not unusual in ancient Rome, and the children remained with their father.

In contrast, lower-class women might choose their own husbands. We have many examples of tombstones belonging to couples who met while they were slaves. Slaves were not allowed to marry, but people formed lasting relationships anyway. A slave who was freed often bought the freedom of his or her partner so that the two could be legally married. Freed slaves and freeborn workers alike might meet future spouses among their coworkers in shops or factories. Among poorer Romans, there was more opportunity for marriage to be based on love and friendship, since political and financial influences were not an issue.

Poorer Romans, however, had to work hard to earn a living. Many women worked only in the home, spinning, weaving, sewing, cooking, cleaning, and raising their children. Sometimes they sold some of the thread they spun or pieces of cloth they wove. Other women might assist their husbands in home-based family busi-

This wife and husband appear to have a close and caring relationship.

nesses. Still others held jobs outside the home or had their own businesses. This may have been especially true of freedwomen, who had often learned and practiced various trades while slaves.

The evidence for Roman working women often makes it difficult to tell if they were slaves, freedwomen, or freeborn women; probably women of all three groups frequently worked side by side, and oftentimes labored alongside men, too. Historians have learned that women worked at a variety of crafts and trades; among others, we know of women who were weavers, menders, dye makers, doctors, midwives, wet nurses, maids, secretaries, hairdressers, dressmakers, perfumers, actresses, dancers, innkeepers, waitresses, bathhouse attendants, shopkeepers, fruit and vegetable sellers, fishmongers, moneylenders, and property owners.

A Roman woman's shop, where she sells poultry, pork, and rabbit

Portrait of a woman from Herculaneum

LITERARY WOMEN

For the most part, literary activities (besides reading) were for men. We do know of a small number of women, though, who were writers. One of these was Sulpicia, who lived in Rome toward the end of the first century B.C.E. Only fragments of a few of Sulpicia's poems survive. Here is a portion of one written in the voice of a young woman, addressed to her guardian, in which she worries about leaving Rome for the countryside, where she will have to spend her birthday apart from her beloved, Cerinthus:

My hateful birthday is at hand, which I must celebrate
   without Cerinthus in the irksome countryside.
What can be sweeter than the City? Or is a country villa
   fit for a girl, or the chilly river in the fields of Arezzo?
Take a rest, Messalla, don't pay so much attention to me;
   journeys, my dear relative, are often untimely.
When I'm taken away, I leave my mind and feelings here,
   since force keeps me from acting as my own master.

Another literary woman was Pamphila of Epidaurus, Greece, who lived around the middle of the first century C.E. The daughter of a learned man, she married a scholar and became extremely interested in history. Pamphila wrote thirty-three books of history, which were much read even a hundred years after her death. They are lost now, but a ninth-century author still knew of Pamphila and summarized her introduction to her work:

> She says that after thirteen years of living with her husband since she was a child, she began to put together these historical materials and recorded what she had learned from her husband during those thirteen years . . . and whatever she happened to hear from anyone else visiting him (for there were many visitors with a reputation for learning). And she added to this what she had read in books.

We can assume—or at least hope—that there were other women like Pamphila who enjoyed the satisfactions of learning.

VI

AN URBAN CHILDHOOD

PRAISE LIFTS THE SPIRIT AND MAKES A CHILD SELF-CONFIDENT,
BUT TOO MUCH PRAISE MAKES HIM INSOLENT AND BAD-TEMPERED.
—SENECA THE YOUNGER, *AN ESSAY ABOUT ANGER*

ll Roman babies were born at home. After birth, the child was laid at its father's feet. If the father picked up the baby, it would be raised by the family. Otherwise the child was exposed—taken outside and left in some public place to die or to be found and raised by someone else. Occasionally an abandoned baby might be taken in by a childless couple who would truly love and care for it. More often, people who picked up these children were slave dealers.

This was one of the harsh facts of life among the Roman poor: parents who already had more children than they could afford to feed sometimes felt they had no choice but to expose their newborn. There were no reliable methods of family planning, no foster-care systems, no adoption agencies. The lack of advanced medical treat-

opposite:
A child grasps a lock of his affectionate father's hair.

125

ments also led people to abandon babies with birth defects. And fathers rejected female infants more often than males, since boys would have a greater ability to contribute to the family income.

Historians cannot be certain how common it was for babies to be abandoned during the first two centuries of the empire. It was an ancient custom, and there were no laws against it. A letter has been found from Roman-ruled Egypt, written in 1 B.C.E. by a husband who had to leave his family to find work. He wrote home to his pregnant wife, "If I receive my pay soon, I will send it up to you. If you have the baby before I return, if it is a boy, let it live; if it is a girl, expose it."

PLAYTIME AND SCHOOL DAYS

Even a baby who wasn't exposed was not sure to survive. Roughly 25 percent of Roman infants died during their first year, and perhaps 25 percent of those who made it to age one died by age ten. So the survival of a healthy child, in a family with the means to care for it, was a source of great joy. Parents generally did all they could to ensure that their children thrived, even taking precautions against supernatural forces. For example, most Roman children wore a *bulla,* a circular pendant made of gold (for the well-off) or leather (for the poor), for protection against evil spirits.

Like children throughout history, Roman children liked toys, games, pets, and sweet treats. Boys and girls in wealthy families, of course, had more opportunities to enjoy these things. Some of the toys available were dolls (made of rags, wood, or bone), model chariots, tops, marbles, hobbyhorses, and wooden swords. There were board games resembling backgammon and checkers. Another game, knucklebones, usually played with the anklebones of goats,

Roman children made toys out of whatever was available. These little boys are playing with nuts.

may have been like jacks. Then there were games similar to hide-and-seek, leapfrog, and blindman's buff. A wide variety of ball games could be enjoyed by children of all ages.

Children's education usually began at home. Parents taught manners, moral principles, and religious beliefs, and probably told stories about their ancestors and great heroes of the past. In prosperous families, trusted slaves also took part in raising and teaching the children. Many wealthy children, particularly boys, were educated at home by private tutors for years. Other boys, and some girls, began attending elementary school around the age of seven.

The school day began as soon as it was light out. Students went home for lunch at midday, but might have more classes afterward. Schools were usually held in shops, small apartments, or public places such as the forum or even on the sidewalk. Students might have chairs, but there were no desks. Sometimes books were used, and the pupils had wooden tablets coated with wax; they used a writing instrument called a stylus to scratch their exercises into the wax. Oftentimes the teacher would simply recite literary passages to the students, who memorized and recited them back. Many teachers beat students who did poorly. Enlightened educators, such as the orator Quintilian, recommended a different approach for teaching a child:

> Let his lessons be fun, let him volunteer answers, let him be praised, and let him learn the pleasure of doing well. If, on occasion, he refuses instruction, bring in someone to serve as a rival, someone with whom he can compete; but let him think that he is doing well more often than not. Encourage him with the rewards or prizes in which his age group delights.

A teacher scolds a late-arriving student while another pupil reads from a scroll.

In elementary school, children learned basic reading, writing, and arithmetic. They also memorized legends, laws, poems, and wise sayings. This was where schooling ended for most Romans—there was no free public education, and most parents could not afford to pay a schoolteacher for more than a few years, if that. Some boys, however, went on to grammar school around the age of ten or eleven. Here they polished their writing ability, studied public speaking and poetry, and learned Greek (if they didn't already know it). They might also study some astronomy, science, music, and philosophy. At the age of fourteen or fifteen, a few boys—usually only those from the upper classes—received advanced training in public speaking and law.

BECOMING AN ADULT

Adult responsibilities came early to most Romans. Slave children and children from very poor families might start working by the age when others were going to elementary school. For example, we have this gravestone inscription for a girl who made women's hairnets: "Viccentia, sweetest daughter, maker of gold nets, who lived for nine years and nine months." Even most boys who went to elementary school probably started working for a living before they were teenagers. If a father practiced a skilled craft or trade, he generally taught it to his sons, who then worked alongside him. Other boys might serve an apprenticeship learning a trade from a neighbor or relative. Many boys had no chance to learn any skills and had to take whatever work they could get.

A boy officially became an adult at around sixteen. The day he came of age was usually one of celebration. First the boy left his *bulla* and his purple-bordered childhood toga at the shrine of his

➷ A GRATEFUL SON ᳭

Horace, who lived during the reign of Augustus, was one of Rome's greatest poets and enjoyed the favor of the emperor himself. This was in spite of the fact that his background was very humble. In the following selection, Horace looks back on his school days and pays tribute to his father for placing him on the road to success:

My father deserves all the credit. For although he was a poor man, with only an infertile plot of land, he was not content to send me to Flavius's school [the school in Horace's hometown] which the burly sons of burly centurions attended, carrying their book-bags and writing tablets slung over their left shoulders. . . . My father had the courage to take his boy to Rome, to have him taught the same skills which any equestrian or senator would have his sons taught. If anyone had seen my clothing or the slaves that attended me, as is the custom in a large city, he would have thought that my expenses were being paid for from an ancestral estate. But my paedagogus [chaperone, usually a slave], my absolutely incorruptible guardian, was my father who accompanied me to school. . . . He didn't make these sacrifices because he worried that someone might criticize him if I became a crier [a town crier, who might also work as an auctioneer] or, like him, a money-collector; nor would I have complained if he hadn't taken me to Rome. But as it is now, he deserves from me unstinting gratitude and praise. I could never be ashamed of such a father, nor do I feel any need, as many people do, to apologize for being a freedman's son.

family's protector deities. Then he put on the pure white toga of manhood. After a visit to the forum, his family and friends gave him a party. If he belonged to the upper classes, he was now able to begin his career in government or business. A lower-class boy could now join the army if he wanted to.

There was no coming-of-age ceremony for girls. After elementary school (if they got to attend at all), they began preparing for marriage, learning the skills they would need to run a household. By the time a girl was a teenager, she was usually married or at least engaged, especially if she belonged to the upper classes. (Daughters of wealthy families tended to marry in their early teens, or even younger; women of the lower classes might not marry till their mid- to late teens.) Her father or guardian chose her husband, who was generally quite a bit older than she was; he might even be in his forties or fifties and have been married before.

The night before her wedding, the bride gave away her toys to younger friends and relatives and laid her *bulla* in the family shrine. Very early on the wedding morning, her mother dressed her in her bridal garments, which included a yellow-orange veil crowned with a wreath of fragrant flowers and herbs. The wedding ceremony took place in the bride's home, with the couple joining hands and stating their consent to be married. Later, a lively torchlit procession escorted the bride to her new home. After she was carried over the threshold (for good luck), two bridesmaids brought in her distaff and spindle, with which she would spin wool, symbolizing her new life as a married woman.

~VII~

REST AND RECREATION

HUNTING, BATHING, GAMING, LAUGHING—THAT IS LIVING.
—MOSAIC PAVEMENT FROM THE FORUM OF TIMGAD

Although the workday began early, for a great many free Romans it ended in midafternoon. Then it was time to visit the baths, where some men might spend most of the rest of the day. Others might go for a stroll after bathing, or meet up with friends at a tavern or snack bar. There they would pass the time drinking, gambling, and talking. Respectable women did not go to taverns, but they could attend dinner parties and similar private social functions. On most holidays—and there were well over one hundred a year—there were free public entertainments that anyone could attend.

opposite: An Egyptian entertainer juggles eggs at a Roman party. This painting is by Lawrence Alma-Tadema, a nineteenth-century artist who was famous for his well-researched portrayals of life in the ancient world.

BOUNTIFUL BANQUETS

Dinnertime arrived in late afternoon. Poor people usually ate very simply, sitting on stools in their apartments and perhaps having little more than porridge and beans, unless they were invited to dine at their patron's home. For well-to-do Romans, giving or attending a dinner party was a favorite form of recreation. These dinners might be relatively small and simple, or they could be lavish banquets with exotic foods and elaborate entertainment. In good weather they were often held outside in the garden or peristyle.

A Roman dining room or outdoor dining area typically contained three couches arranged around a low table. Diners reclined, leaning on their left elbows, three to a couch. They ate with spoons, knives, and their fingers. Slaves waited on them and brought them water for hand washing whenever necessary. For some special outdoor dinners, the couches were set around a garden pool, and the guests selected morsels of food from boat-shaped floating dishes.

A Roman dinner generally had three courses, but there could be several dishes in each course. First came appetizers, which were often egg dishes, fish, and raw vegetables. The main course featured meats and cooked vegetables. Choices for dessert included fruit, pastries, and cakes. The usual drink was wine.

The entertainment during and after a meal depended on the host's wealth and tastes. Many diners were satisfied simply with good conversation. Slaves often provided music while guests were eating. Between courses there might be performances by singers, dancers, actors, or acrobats. Upper-class men with literary interests often held recitations as part of the after-dinner entertainment. They would read aloud from their own writings, or from the works of famous authors.

❧ EAT LIKE A ROMAN ❧

Here is a simple menu similar to what a reasonably well-off Roman might have eaten for dinner. If you also want to drink like a Roman, you can serve grape juice instead of wine, but it should be at room temperature.

Gustatio (Appetizers)
- Scrambled eggs topped with tuna, finely chopped raw onions,
  and fresh rosemary.
- Fresh watercress with a dressing made of Worcestershire sauce (1 T.), red-wine or cider vinegar (1 T.), olive oil (3 T.), and black pepper to taste.
  (The Worcestershire sauce is a substitution for a sauce made from pickled
  fish that the Romans used in much of their cooking.)

Prima Mensa (Main Course)
- Small sausages served on a bed of couscous or Cream of Wheat.
  (Romans ate a lot of wheat porridge and similar grain dishes.)
- Steamed carrot strips, reheated with a little olive oil and cumin.
- Cooked white beans with bacon crumbled on top.
  (Fava beans would be most authentic, but you could use
  cannellini, or white kidney beans, instead.)

Secunda Mensa (Dessert)
- Roasted chestnuts (these can be bought canned) dipped in honey.
- Fresh pears and apple slices sprinkled with cinnamon and raisins.

Clients were expected to attend recitations by their patron (and to praise him enthusiastically), and many men felt that going to recitations was a boring duty. Others, however, looked forward to these literary dinners, as Pliny the Younger wrote in one of his letters: "I scarcely ever miss a recitation. Of course, usually the people reciting are friends of mine; for there is almost no one who is fond of literary studies who is not also fond of me."

THE GAMES

The Romans referred to several different kinds of events as *ludi,* or games, including plays and other theatrical presentations. Plays were modeled on Greek comedies and tragedies, and only men acted in them. Pantomimes were more popular but also less respectable because they included female performers and appealed to the senses with music, dance, beautiful costumes and scenery, and lively action. Pantomimes may have been a little like ballets, since the performers acted out stories—usually based on familiar myths and legends—without using words. Quintilian wrote about how skilled and expressive the performers could be: "Their hands demand and promise, they summon and dismiss; they translate horror, fear, joy, sorrow. . . . They excite and they calm. They implore and they approve. They possess a power of imitation which replaces words."

Rome's oldest and most beloved form of popular entertainment was chariot racing. Races were held on a narrow oval track in a large roofless building called a circus. By the end of the second century there were eight circuses in and around the city of Rome alone; the largest of these, the Circus Maximus, had room for 250,000 spectators. In cities throughout the empire, chariot racing was highly organized. There were four racing factions, or teams,

named after the colors of their uniforms: Greens, Blues, Reds, and Whites. The same four colors were used wherever there was a circus, even though, for example, the Greens in Rome had a different owner and drivers than the Greens in Pompeii. The faction owners owned not only the chariots, horses, and stables, but also most of the drivers. Every faction had die-hard fans who sat together in the circus to cheer for their team and boo against the other factions. Sometimes fans of different factions even got into fistfights during a race.

Chariot racing was an exciting sport. The course was long and narrow, with tight left-hand turns at each end. The lightweight chariots, made of wicker or wood, might be pulled by two to ten horses, although most races were for four-horse chariots. The drivers used whips to urge their horses through seven laps around the track. (In the Circus Maximus, this made for a race of about 2.5 miles.) Crashes, injuries, and even deaths among both horses and drivers were common—but for the spectators, this element of danger only added to the excitement.

The excitement of a chariot race in the Circus Maximus is brought to life by a modern artist.

A CELEBRITY

Imperial Rome didn't have movie stars or rock stars, but it did have sports stars. Successful gladiators and charioteers became wildly popular celebrities. Although they were usually slaves or freedmen, they were admired by people at all levels of society. Wealthy fans—including some emperors—showered their favorites with gifts and invited them to fancy dinner parties and other social events.

Part of what made these stars of the arena and racetrack seem so glamorous, their lives so thrilling, was the danger involved in their professions. Every time a gladiator or chariot driver won a fight or a race, he was victorious not only over his opponents but also over death. Toward the end of the first century, a driver named Scorpus was one of the biggest stars ever, having won 2,048 races. But his good fortune couldn't last: at the age of twenty-six, he was killed in a crash on the racetrack. The poet Martial wrote this epitaph for him:

Here I lie, Scorpus, the pride of the noisy Circus, the darling of Rome, wildly cheered, but short-lived. Spiteful Lachesis* snatched me away in my twenty-sixth year. She counted my victories, not my years, and decided that I was an old man.

Alas, what a crime! You were cheated of your youth, Scorpus. You have fallen and died. Too soon have you harnessed the dark horses of death. Why did the finish line of the race, which you time and again hastened to cross, quickly covering the distance in your chariot, now become the finish of your life?

*the goddess who decided the length of a person's life

This detail from a mosaic shows a wild-animal fight in an amphitheater, with a gladiator killing a leopard.

Even bloodier games took place in the empire's amphitheaters. These nearly circular open-air stadiums were the scenes of gladiator combats and wild-animal fights. Gladiators were usually slaves or prisoners of war.* They were trained to fight in specific styles; for example, a *retiarius* was a gladiator who fought with a net and trident, while a Thracian used a curved sword and round shield. Most fights were not necessarily to the death, although a gladiator certainly could be killed or mortally injured during the course of combat. On the other hand, amphitheater shows also included executions, in which condemned criminals were sent to fight gladiators or wild animals. Those who received this sentence went into the arena unarmed, and they did not come out alive.

One of the world's most famous buildings, the Colosseum in Rome, was an amphitheater. When the emperor Titus opened it in 80 C.E., he sponsored one hundred days of elaborate spectacles, as reported by the senator and historian Dio Cassius:

> There was a battle between cranes and also between four elephants; animals both tame and wild were slain to the number of nine thousand; and women (not those of any

*Once in a while a freeborn man who could find no other work would become a gladiator. Also, some slaves who were freed after several years as gladiators continued to fight in the arena, charging high fees for doing so.

prominence, however) took part in despatching them. As for the men, several fought in single combat and several groups contended together both in infantry and naval battles. For Titus suddenly filled this same theatre with water and brought in horses and bulls and some other domesticated animals that had been taught to behave in the liquid element just as on land. He also brought in people on ships, who engaged in a sea-fight there.

Not all Romans enjoyed these types of events. Seneca the Younger, for one, was highly critical of their influence. He wrote to a friend, "There is nothing more harmful to one's character than attendance at some spectacle, because vices more easily creep into your soul while you are being entertained. When I return home from some spectacle, I am greedier, more aggressive. . . . I am more cruel and inhumane." Most people today would agree with Seneca—but for a great many ancient Romans, it seems that amphitheater events gave them a welcome escape from their own poverty and powerlessness.

·VIII·

SURVIVING IN THE CITY

IF THERE COULD BE SOME WAY OF STOPPING HOUSES IN ROME
CATCHING FIRE THE WHOLE TIME, I SHOULD CERTAINLY SELL ALL MY
PROPERTY IN THE COUNTRY AND BUY URBAN PROPERTY.
—AULUS GELLIUS, *ATTIC NIGHTS*

A Roman city could be a difficult and even dangerous place to live. Crime, crowding, noise, pollution, poverty, unemployment—cities everywhere have suffered from such problems. In the ancient world, some of these troubles were especially bad. For example, with no streetlights of any kind, it was very easy for thieves to sneak up on pedestrians at night. Not surprisingly, Roman city dwellers rarely went out after dark; if they had to, slaves or hired boys carried torches to light the way. Nighttime travelers who were poor rarely had these options. And thieves were not the only hazard, since it was difficult for people to even see where they were going in the darkness.

Along with kitchen garbage and other trash, urban pollution included sewage and animal manure. These wastes accumulated in

Apothecaries' shops, like this one in Rome, sold various medicinal substances, only some of which were effective.

alleyway cesspits and dung heaps, posing a constant threat to public health—and a persistent assault to the nose. While Rome and many other cities did have wonderful sewer systems for the time, the sewers mainly drained bathhouses and public lavatories, and they emptied the wastewater and untreated sewage into the nearest river.

The water system, excellent as it was coming from the countryside, also posed a danger; since lead pipes were frequently used, it is likely that a great number of Roman city dwellers suffered from lead poisoning. Lead was also an ingredient in some women's cosmetics—even makeup had its perils. Many Romans, however, did realize that lead was harmful; Vitruvius wrote, "Water ought by no means to be conducted in lead pipes, if we want to have it wholesome." Unfortunately, Vitruvius's advice was largely ignored.

Disease was inescapable for rich and poor alike, although the poor were especially susceptible to illnesses caused by malnutrition and poor sanitation. But even for the wealthy, there were no vaccines, antibiotics, or advanced surgical procedures. There were also no standards of education for doctors. Good ones learned their profession by apprenticing to skilled physicians. Anyone, however, could claim to be a doctor, without any training at all. The most experienced doctors were still unable to cure a great number of illnesses. The average life expectancy for ancient Romans was only twenty-seven years.

℘ THE ANNOYING SIDE ℘
OF CITY LIFE

Juvenal may have come from a city about eighty miles southeast of Rome. After serving a term as *duovir* in his hometown, he moved to the capital, where he lived through many personal and political ups and downs. Between the years 110 and 127, he wrote his sixteen *Satires*, poems that exaggerated and ridiculed the annoyances and follies he witnessed every day in Rome. Here is a selection from Juvenal's third *Satire*, in which he complains about the noise and crowds that sometimes made city life nearly unbearable:

> Most sick men here die from insomnia (of course
> their illness starts with food undigested, clogging
> the burning stomach)—for in any rented room
> rest is impossible. It costs money to sleep in Rome.
> There is the root of the sickness. The movement of heavy waggons
> through narrow streets, the oaths of stalled cattle-drovers
> would break the sleep of a deaf man or a lazy walrus.
> On a morning call the crowd gives way before the passage
> of a millionaire carried above their heads in a litter,
> reading the while he goes, or writing, or sleeping unseen:
> for a man becomes sleepy with closed windows and comfort.
> Yet he'll arrive before us. We have to fight our way
> through a wave in front, and behind we are pressed by a huge mob
> shoving our hips; an elbow hits us here and a pole
> there, now we are smashed by a beam, now biffed by a barrel.
> Our legs are thick with mud, our feet are crushed by large
> ubiquitous shoes, a soldier's hobnail rests on our toe.

CATASTROPHE!

Cities, with their crowded conditions, were highly vulnerable to epidemics and other disasters. One of the calamities most feared by city dwellers was fire. Spreading easily from building to building, a fire could wipe out whole neighborhoods in a very short time. Rome itself suffered several catastrophic fires. The worst one occurred in 64 C.E., during the reign of the emperor Nero. Tacitus described it:

> The blaze in its fury ran first through the level portions of the city, then rising to the hills, while it again devastated every place below them, it outstripped all preventive measures. . . . At last, after five days, an end was put to the conflagration . . . by the destruction of all buildings on a vast space, so that the violence of the fire was met by clear ground and an open sky. But before people laid aside their fears, the flames returned, with no less fury this second time. . . . Rome, indeed, is divided into fourteen districts, four of which remained uninjured, three were leveled to the ground, while in the other seven were left only a few shattered, half-burnt relics of houses.

Natural disasters also struck Roman cities from time to time. Early in the first century, the city of Sardis in Asia Minor was hit by a huge earthquake. The rebuilding of Sardis took more than a century. An earthquake that struck Pompeii in 62 did so much damage that some people thought this city should just be abandoned. It wasn't, and seventeen years later Pompeii and the neighboring town of Herculaneum were the victims of one of history's most famous disasters, the eruption of Mount Vesuvius. Both cities were buried under deep layers of volcanic debris. The catastrophe, however, preserved the two towns in an almost untouched state. Since the eighteenth century, archaeologists have been carefully unearthing and studying them, revealing ever more information about urban life in the Roman Empire.

REDUCING THE RISKS

Emperors sent relief money and gave other assistance to cities hit by disaster. For example, after the earthquake in Sardis, the emperor Tiberius pledged a huge sum of money for rebuilding and cancelled the Sardians' tax payments for five years. The emperor Titus arranged housing and financial help for many of the people who

The ruins of the Forum of Trajan in Rome. The slightly curved structure toward the back is all that remains of Trajan's Market. Even where there were no fires or natural disasters, time has taken its toll on the cities of the Roman Empire.

A cast of one of the victims of Vesuvius, which looms in the background

◈ EYEWITNESS TO DISASTER ◈

Pliny the Elder, admiral and famous scholar, commanded the Roman fleet that was based about nineteen miles across the Bay of Naples from Pompeii. His seventeen-year-old nephew, Pliny the Younger, was visiting him when Vesuvius erupted. Later Pliny the Younger wrote an eyewitness account of the disaster, beginning, "On 24 August, in the early afternoon, my mother drew his [Pliny the Elder's] attention to a cloud of unusual size. . . . Its general appearance . . . [was] like an umbrella pine, for it rose to a great height on a sort of trunk and then split off into branches. . . . Sometimes it looked white, sometimes blotched and dirty."

The admiral's scientific curiosity was awakened, and he set sail across the bay for a closer look. The expedition turned into a rescue mission, with several ships working to carry people away from the catastrophic eruption. "And now cinders, which grew thicker and hotter the nearer he approached, fell into the ships, then pumice stones, too, with stones blackened, scorched, and cracked by fire. Then the sea ebbed suddenly from under them, while the shore was blocked by landslips from the mountains."

Pliny the Elder commanded his ship to land about four miles south of Pompeii. Unable to put to sea again because of fierce wind and waves, he took refuge for the night in a friend's villa. By early morning, "the courtyard giving access to his room was full of ashes mixed with pumice stones, so that its level had risen, and if he had stayed in the room any longer, he would never have got out. The buildings were now shaking with violent shocks, and seemed to be swaying to and fro, as if they were torn from their foundations." Back at the naval base, Pliny the Younger and his mother experienced these same tremors and fled their house:

The coaches that we had ordered out, though upon the most level ground, were sliding to and fro and could not be kept steady. . . . Then we beheld the sea sucked back, leaving many sea animals captive on the dry sand. . . . A black and dreadful cloud bursting out in gusts of igneous serpentine vapor now and again yawned open to reveal long, fantastic flames, resembling flashes of lightning but much larger. Soon afterward, the cloud began to descend upon the earth and cover the sea. Ashes now fell upon us, though as yet in no great quantity. I looked behind me; darkness came rolling over the land after us like a torrent. I proposed, while we yet could see, to turn aside, lest we should be knocked down in the road by a crowd that followed us, and trampled to death in the dark. We had scarce sat down when darkness overspread us. . . . You could hear the shrieks of women and crying children and the shouts of men; some were seeking their children, others their parents; some praying to die, from the very fear of dying; many lifting their hands to the gods; but the greater part imagining that there were no gods left anywhere, that the last and eternal night was come upon the world.

This cloud of ash and poisonous gas thinned out as it crossed the bay, and so Pliny the Younger lived to tell the tale. His uncle was not so lucky. He had left the villa and gone to the shore to see if there was any way to escape. Surrounded by the dark cloud from the volcano, choking on the sulfurous fumes, Pliny the Elder collapsed on the beach and died, one of Vesuvius's thousands of victims.

fled their homes when Vesuvius began to erupt. Other emperors, too, looked for various ways to improve life in the empire's cities.

For the city of Rome, Augustus established not only the police force-like urban cohort but also the *vigiles*. These were night watchmen and, more importantly, trained firefighters. There were 3,500 (later increased to 7,000) men in the *vigiles*, and some of them also did duty in Ostia, the port city that served Rome. The commander of the *vigiles* was an equestrian, but the firefighters themselves were freedmen.

The great fire of 64 showed that some blazes were too huge even for the *vigiles* to handle, so Nero decreed new fire safety regulations. These included limiting the height of apartment buildings, requiring fireproof stone to be used in a large part of all new construction, leaving more open space in front of buildings, and keeping firefighting equipment available in the courtyards of all residences. Many other cities followed Rome's model in setting up fire safety laws and firefighting units.

Another urban problem that demanded attention was poverty. The patron-client relationship was a kind of welfare system, since patrons' gifts of food and money helped many of the working poor as well as the unemployed. But too often this was not enough. Many poor citizens relied on a monthly distribution of free grain by the government. The emperors did their best to help assure the timely delivery of large amounts of grain to Rome—there was always a danger of riots if the supply ran low. As an additional measure to keep the populace happy, emperors occasionally handed out gifts of money, food, and clothes.

In the second century the emperor Trajan established a welfare program specifically to help poor children. Every year a sum of money was distributed to various Italian cities for the benefit of these children. Many other wealthy Romans also set up charitable funds, like a man from North Africa who gave his city a large amount of money so that "there may be fed and maintained each year 300 boys and 300 girls." Among other charitable acts, Pliny the Younger donated funds to his hometown in northern Italy to support poor children and to establish a school, a library, and a bathhouse. Pliny and those like him felt that since they were fortunate enough to be wealthy and educated, it was their duty to use at least some of their resources for the public good.

This attitude toward charity and public service is one of the great legacies of the Roman Empire. Looking back, we may be able to learn from the Romans how to solve some of the problems that confront our cities and our society today. Sometimes the history of the empire shows us possible solutions; at other times it warns us what to avoid. The Romans laid much of the foundation for our modern city-based lifestyle. To know their story is to know ourselves all the better.

THE COUNTRYSIDE

· I ·
THE EMPIRE'S SUPPORT SYSTEM

THEN LET ME LOVE THE COUNTRY, THE RIVERS RUNNING
THROUGH VALLEYS, THE STREAMS AND WOODLANDS. . . .
GIVE ME BROAD FIELDS AND SWEEPING RIVERS,
LOFTY MOUNTAIN RANGES IN DISTANT LANDS,
COLD PRECIPITOUS VALLEYS, WHERE I MAY LIE BENEATH
THE ENORMOUS DARKNESS OF THE BRANCHES!
—VIRGIL, *GEORGICS*

When we think about ancient Rome, we usually picture life in the great city itself, and in all the other cities of the empire. Roman civilization was focused on urban life—even the word "civilization" comes from one of the Romans' words for "city," *civis.* Most people in the Roman Empire, however, did not live in cities. They lived in rural areas: on scattered farmsteads, in villages and small towns, or on plantation-like farming estates. Although history has largely ignored these people, their work as farmers, herders, spinners, weavers—among other rural occupations—was essential to the strength and well-being of the Roman Empire.

opposite:
A country dweller carries chickens and a basket of eggs to a town market.

153

A ROMAN IDEAL

According to legend, the founder of Rome was Romulus, a shepherd. Many of his followers were shepherds, too, and farmers. The early city, in fact, was a union of farming villages scattered over seven neighboring hills. Even after Rome was well on its way to becoming the greatest city on the Italian peninsula, the Romans thought of themselves as a nation of simple, honest, hardworking farmers. After Augustus came to power, and Rome dominated the Mediterranean world, Romans still looked back with pride on their rural traditions. As the great poet Virgil wrote of this heritage, "Through this, Rome became the fairest thing on earth."

The countryside and rural life were celebrated not only by Virgil but by many other poets, including Horace, Tibullus, and Martial. The authors Varro and Columella composed treatises on agriculture. The author-statesman Pliny the Younger often wrote about his enjoyment of his country villas and his concerns about his farming estates. The historian Tacitus was one of many Romans who felt that society had become too "citified"—overly sophisticated, even decadent—and looked back on the "good old days" of the rural past. Horace, for example, says this about the great Romans of former times:

> Those were the sons of farmers and soldiers too—
> tough males, accustomed, mattock in hand, to break
> hard clods, and bring home logs for firing
> under the eye of a mother stern and
> strong-willed.

Such authors—nearly all wealthy men who lived, at least part-time, in the city—idealized country life. Unfortunately, we have very

⤙ HAPPINESS IN THE COUNTRYSIDE ↝

Publius Vergilius Maro, known in English as Virgil or Vergil, lived from 70 to 19 B.C.E. Ever since his death, he has been regarded as the greatest of all Roman poets. He was born in a small village in northern Italy, but lived for some years in Rome, where he became acquainted with the emperor Augustus. Virgil always retained a love for the countryside, however, and a respect for farmers, although he sometimes idealized their lives. Following is a selection from one of his *Georgics,* a group of poems he wrote about rural life.

Happy—even too happy, if they knew their bliss—
are farmers, who receive, far from the clash of war,
an easy livelihood from the just and generous earth.
Although they own no lofty mansion with proud gates,
from every hall disgorging floods of visitors, . . .
still they sleep without care and live without deceit,
rich with various plenty, peaceful in broad expanses,
in grottoes, lakes of living water, cool dark glens,
with the brute music of cattle, soft sleep at noon
beneath the trees: they have forests, the lairs of wild game;
they have sturdy sons, hard-working, content with little,
the sanctity of God, and reverence for the old.
Justice, quitting this earth, left her last footprints there.

little written material from the common people whose lives centered on farming and other rural work. Few of these people knew how to read and write, and most of them worked too long and hard to take time for recording their experiences. Once in a while, though, we do hear the voice of someone from the countryside, as in this inscription from the tombstone of a North African man:

> From the day of my birth I have lived by working my land; neither my land nor I has ever had a rest. . . . Twelve years' harvests I cut under the raging sun, . . . and for eleven years I commanded teams of harvesters. . . . Hard work, and contentment with little, finally brought me a home with a farmstead, and my home lacks nothing in wealth. Furthermore, my career has achieved the rewards of office; . . . from a poor farm boy I actually became a censor [an official in the local government]. I have seen my children and my grandchildren grow up around me, and I have enjoyed years distinguished by the merits of my career. . . . Thus has he deserved to die who has lived honourably.

SUSTAINING THE CITY

In the ancient world, country and city generally had a very close relationship. Most cities controlled outlying rural areas, which depended on the cities for protection and supplied them with grain, vegetables, honey, wool, and other agricultural products. Usually there were many people who lived in cities but left them each day to work in the nearby fields. In numerous cases, there were fields, orchards, and pastures even within city walls.

Rome itself, with more than a million people, was so large that

Hunters load a deer and an ostrich onto a ship for transport to Rome.

the surrounding region could not support it alone. More than six million sacks of grain a year were required to feed the city's residents. This grain was grown mainly in Sicily and parts of North Africa, expecially Egypt. North Africa was also home to extensive olive orchards, as was Spain. Rome imported olive oil from both regions to meet the needs of its population. The oil was used in everything from cooking to lamp fuel, to soaps and body lotions. Wine was another item exported from Spain to Rome in great quantity. Some of the best wines enjoyed by upper-class Romans, however, were produced in the vineyards scattered over the Italian countryside. Most of the pork and wool used in Rome came

THE COUNTRYSIDE

from the province of Cisalpine Gaul, the region of Italy just south of the Alps.

All over the empire, products flowed into cities from rural areas. The countryside provided a wide array of goods, from meat and milk to linen and dyestuffs to precious metals and building materials. Numerous cities, especially in the eastern empire, were as dependent on imported grain as Rome was. In many of these places, the surrounding region easily could have produced grain—but instead the land was used for the more profitable crops of grapes and olives. Basic food supplies often had to travel a long distance from country to city.

Another way in which the countryside played a supporting role to cities was by providing a place where busy urbanites could relax and "get away from it all" for a time. As Martial wrote, "Do you ask why I often make for my little farm in arid Nomentum [a small town northeast of Rome], and the untidy household of my villa? In the city . . . poor men have no place where they can think or stay quiet. . . . Whenever I'm worn out with anxiety, and want to sleep, I go to my farm." Rome (like other Mediterranean cities) was not only noisy and bustling, but in the summer it could be unbearably hot, so wealthy people migrated to villas in the hills or near the sea. Many villas were not simply "vacation homes" for their owners but were part of working farms. Agricultural products and the money from their sale were, in fact, the main source of wealth for many upper-class Romans.

CONQUERED COUNTRYSIDE

Rome was the mightiest military power in the Western world. Its conquests gave it control over numerous diverse areas. Some parts of the empire were thickly urbanized, such as Italy, Greece, southern Spain, and the coasts of Asia Minor. Other provinces were far more rural, particularly in the north and west, with cities fewer and farther between. It was in these less urbanized areas, generally speaking, that the bulk of Rome's troops were stationed.

The Roman army had two main divisions, the legions and the auxiliaries. Legionary soldiers were all Roman citizens, mostly from Italy and what are now Spain, southern France, and Turkey. The auxiliaries were soldiers recruited from the provinces. Some were citizens, but most earned Roman citizenship at the completion of their military service. The majority of legionnaires were foot soldiers, while auxiliaries often had specialized skills, such as fighting on horseback or using bows or slings. Some auxiliary units were made up of men required to fight for Rome as part of a treaty agreement between their people and the empire. In any case, up until about the middle of the second century, auxiliaries rarely served in their home province. So, for example, the soldiers who kept order for the empire in Britain were from what are now the Netherlands, northeastern Greece, Algeria, and Ukraine. When auxiliaries and legionnaires were discharged from the army, they often settled in towns or farming communities in the province where they had been stationed. This was one of the most important ways that Roman culture spread through the countryside of conquered territories.

Roman rule brought order and peace to conquered areas, but at a price. Many thought this price was too high, although few had the courage to speak out. Roman soldiers were never far away, ready to deal with troublemakers at a moment's notice. But in the 80s C.E., the empire met strong resistance when it tried to push its rule into northern Britain. The historian Tacitus put the following speech

A warrior north of the empire's frontier defends his home from a Roman soldier.

into the mouth of a British leader named Calgacus, rallying his warriors against the Romans in what is now northeastern Scotland:

Up until this day, we who live in this last strip of land and last home of liberty have been protected by our very remoteness. . . . But now the farthest limits of Britain have been opened up. . . . Beyond us, there are no tribes, nothing except waves and rocks and, more dangerous than these, the Romans, whose oppression you have in vain tried to escape by obedience and submission. Plunderers of the world they are, and now that there is no more territory left to occupy their hands which have already laid the world waste, they are scouring the seas. If the enemy is rich, they are greedy; if the enemy is poor, they are power-hungry. . . . Alone of all men they covet rich nations and poor nations with equal passion. They rob, they slaughter, they plunder—and they call it "empire." Where they make a waste-land, they call it "peace."

Nature has planned that each man love his children and family very dearly. Yet these are torn from us . . . to be slaves elsewhere. . . . Our possessions and our money are consumed in providing tribute; our farmland and our yearly produce are consumed in providing them with grain; our very bodies and hands are worn down while clearing forests and swamps for them, who beat and insult us.

II
COUNTRY COMMUNITIES

Hail, earthly paradise, mighty mother of crops
and mother of men!
—Virgil praising Italy in the *Georgics*

There was great diversity in the Roman Empire. This applied not only to people and their customs but also to their environments and natural resources. Britain was damp and chilly, North Africa hot and dry. Germany was heavily wooded; in Greece the terrain was rough and rocky. Along the Nile River in Egypt, the flat, fertile land was perfect for growing wheat; Italian hillsides were covered with grapevines and olive trees. In Spain the earth held rich deposits of gold and other metals, while marble could be quarried from many parts of Asia Minor.

How people lived in the countryside naturally depended on climate, the quality of the land, and the available resources. We also need to remember that a great deal of change has occurred since

opposite:
A wealthy woman, surrounded by servants, enjoys the garden at her villa in North Africa.

163

Rome ruled the Mediterranean world. For example, forests covered much more of western Europe in Roman times than today, and areas in North Africa that are now desert were then green with orchards of olive trees.

A VARIETY OF VILLAGES

Many country people lived in villages. Some rural settlements might have only a handful of houses, occupied by farm families that worked the surrounding fields. Other villages might be home not only to farmers but also to craftspeople, and there might be an inn and other amenities. Pliny the Younger mentioned in a letter to one of his friends that the village near his seaside villa had three public bathhouses.

Small towns were also important to the countryside. Farmers could sell some of their produce at markets in these towns and could use the money to buy things that they couldn't make themselves or get from village craftspeople. Virgil gave this description of a country dweller's visit to his local market town: "Often the farmer drives the sluggish donkey, loading its sides with oil or cheap apples, while on the return trip he brings back from town a grooved millstone or a lump of dark pitch."

In much of the Roman Empire, villages were often made up entirely of native people living in their traditional ways. For instance, the first four books of the New Testament of the Bible frequently describe village life in the province of Judaea (roughly, modern Israel), where fishing was an important part of the rural economy. Throughout the empire, there could be a good deal of variety even in the basic layout of country communities: as an example, many British villages were surrounded by wide ditches, while North African villages were often walled and fortified with towers.

⊸ LIFE ON THE EMPIRE'S FRINGES ⌀

In mainland Europe, the Roman Empire's northern boundary was the Danube River. Across it lived a number of Germanic tribes. Rome tried many times to conquer German territory, but even when it succeeded, these lands were hard to hold on to. Only in the west, along the Rhine River, did the empire manage to maintain a presence in Germany. This area was a military zone for many years, then in 90 C.E. became the provinces of Upper and Lower Germany. Not long afterward, Tacitus wrote his *Germania,* a study of the lands and peoples of the Rhine-Danube region. Here is an excerpt, in which Tacitus describes the Germans' typical communities:

It is well known that none of the German tribes live in cities, that even individually they do not permit houses to touch each other: they live separated and scattered, according as spring-water, meadow, or grove appeals to each man: they lay out their villages not, after our fashion, with buildings contiguous [touching each other] and connected; every one keeps a clear space round his house, whether it be a precaution against the chances of fire, or just ignorance of building. They have not even learned to use quarry-stone or tiles: the timber they use for all purposes is unshaped, and stops short of all ornament or attraction: certain buildings are smeared with a stucco bright and glittering enough to be a substitute for paint and frescoes. . . .

Land is taken up by a village as a whole, in quantity according to the number of the cultivators: they then distribute it among themselves on the basis of rank, such distribution being made easy by the extent of domain occupied. They change the arable land yearly, and there is still land to spare, for they do not strain the fertility and resources of the soil. . . . Grain is the only harvest required of the land; accordingly the year itself is not divided into as many parts as with us: winter, spring, summer have a meaning and name; of autumn the name alike and bounties are unknown.

GREAT ESTATES

In both Italy and the provinces, large tracts of land were owned by the emperor—and all of Egypt belonged to him. Each of the emperor's estates was run by an official called a procurator, who was often a freed slave. The procurator usually rented out parts of the estate to tenant farmers. Sometimes extensive parcels of land were rented to one person. This "lessee-in-chief" or chief tenant would be allowed to have part of the estate farmed for himself, and he would sublet the rest to humbler tenant farmers. The emperor's estates often incorporated entire villages, as this inscription from North Africa shows:

> Anyone living within the estate of Villa Magna Variana, that is, in the village of Siga, is permitted to bring those fields which are unsurveyed under cultivation. . . . Of the crops produced on such land they [the tenants] must in accordance with the Mancian Law deliver shares . . . to the chief lessees or bailiffs of this estate as follows. . . . one third of the wheat from the threshing floor, one third of the barley from the threshing floor, one fourth of the beans from the threshing floor, one third of the wine from the vat, one third of the oil extracted, one *sextarius* [a little more than a pint] of honey per hive.

Other wealthy Romans also had great landholdings—it is said that at one point, half the province of Africa (modern Tunisia and northwestern Libya) was owned by six men. This was an extreme case, however, and most estates were not so vast. Large landowners generally lived in the cities, not on their estates. But on most estates

A portion of the emperor Hadrian's magnificent country estate at Tivoli (fifteen miles outside Rome), reconstructed in a scale model

they would have a villa, which they visited from time to time. Many wealthy Romans had a network of villas throughout Italy, so that they and their friends would have places to stay while traveling, since there were few decent hotels. The estates themselves were run by stewards or bailiffs and worked by slaves, tenant farmers, sharecroppers, or some combination of these. Italian estates produced mainly wine, olive oil, and grain, but in some parts of the peninsula great tracts of land were devoted to cattle ranching.

The poet Horace had a fairly modest estate, about thirty miles from Rome. He spent as much time in his villa there as he could—"I always leave with a sigh whenever loathsome business drags me back to Rome," he wrote. He rented part of his estate to five tenant farmers, each family living in its own cottage and working a plot of land. The rest of the estate was worked by eight slaves, overseen by a foreman. Its produce (including the profits from sales) directly supported the poet. He had grain fields, a vegetable garden, an orchard, a vineyard, an olive grove, a wood, pastureland, and cattle, sheep, and goats. The countryside around Horace's estate was still quite wild: once while rambling alone in the forest, he unexpectedly came upon a wolf—luckily for both, the poet was unarmed, and the wolf soon went its own way.

THE COUNTRYSIDE

FRONTIER FORTS

Roman legions were headquartered in leading provincial cities. Soldiers, however—both legionnaires and auxiliaries—manned outposts and forts that were strung through the countryside or along the empire's boundaries. One such frontier was Hadrian's Wall, which divided the province of Britannia from what is now Scotland. Built into the wall were sixteen or seventeen large fortresses, each manned by some five hundred auxiliaries. There were also smaller fortresses called milecastles, placed roughly one mile apart, which garrisoned around thirty men and also served as gatehouses. Watchtowers rose approximately every third of a mile along the wall.

Wherever soldiers were stationed, villages soon came into being. Some local people wanted the protection of the Roman soldiers, for in many places bandits and raiders threatened the safety

Roman soldiers building a fortified camp during the course of the emperor Trajan's war to conquer Dacia (modern Romania)

of the countryside. Others were more interested in earning money by supplying the soldiers with goods and services. Until 197 C.E. rank-and-file legionnaires and auxiliaries were not allowed to marry, but often they had unofficial wives who, with their children, naturally wanted to live as close to the army camp as possible. So a typical settlement near a military base might include a tavern, a few craftspeople's workshops, a marketplace, and the homes of soldiers' families and of people who farmed the surrounding countryside. Over time, many such settlements grew into full-fledged towns and cities.

Not all rural people, however, lived in villages, on villas, or near military posts. In almost every province there were at least some freeholders who occupied scattered or isolated farmsteads, working land that often had been passed down through families for generations. And in North Africa and a few other areas on the empire's edges, many groups carried on an age-old nomadic lifestyle. They traveled from place to place, following the grazing patterns of their animals. At the same time they played a role in village culture by trading products from their herds for grain, vegetables, and the like. In addition, nomads provided temporary, seasonal labor on many farms.

III

COUNTRY HOMES

IF WE MUST LIVE IN PERFECT HARMONY WITH NATURE
AND FIRST DISCOVER A SITE ON WHICH TO BUILD OUR HOME,
WHAT PLACE IS BETTER THAN THE HEAVENLY COUNTRYSIDE?
—HORACE, *EPISTLES*

 ural people lived in various ways in different parts of the empire. This can be seen in housing, artwork, religious practices, and clothing. For example, peasant men in Britain and Germany often wore woolen breeches and hooded hip-length cloaks that fastened up the front. Male North African farmworkers, in contrast, wore lightweight tunics that reached to just above their knees. In Syria, the traditional dress included baggy trousers that fitted closely at the ankles. The poet Ovid described some of the seminomadic men who lived near the mouth of the Danube this way: "With [animal] skins and loose breeches they keep off the evils of the cold; their shaggy faces are protected with long locks." These men's long hair and beards contrasted sharply with the short hair and clean-shaven faces generally favored in Italy by town dwellers and country folk alike.

opposite:
A home on the bank of the Nile River in Roman-ruled Egypt

171

HUMBLE ABODES

The architect Vitruvius noted that the native people in different parts of the empire each had traditional building styles. Houses in what are now France and Spain, he said, were roofed with oak shingles or thatch. On the south coast of the Black Sea, tall log cabins were typical. "On the other hand," Vitruvius continued,

> the Phrygians [of central Asia Minor], who live in an open country, have no forests and consequently lack timber. They therefore select a natural hillock, run a trench through the middle of it, dig passages, and extend the interior space as widely as the site admits. Over it they build a pyramidal roof of logs fastened together, and this they cover with reeds and brushwood, heaping up very high mounds of earth above their dwellings. Thus their fashion in houses makes their winters very warm and their summers very cool.

We know from other evidence that British houses were often round and constructed of wattle and daub, with steep, conical thatched roofs. Egyptian villagers built their homes of mud brick, with flat roofs. The Romans rarely interfered with these various building traditions, but in their own settlements, whether in Italy or the provinces, they built in their own style.

Roman country houses were mainly rectangular in shape. They might be constructed of stone, wood, concrete with a brick facing, or a combination of these materials. Roofs were usually covered with clay tiles. The poorest homes had floors of hard-packed earth; people who were more comfortably off had wood, stone, or tile underfoot. Walls were often plastered or whitewashed inside and out.

A simple home or cottage was typically partitioned into a few small rooms, one leading into another. Archaeologists in Italy have found the remains of a humble farmhouse with an interior measuring approximately thirty-three feet by fifteen feet. There is evidence that farm animals sheltered in one part of the house—a common living arrangement in many places in the past. The animals were protected from thieves and the weather, and when it was cold, their body heat helped warm the house for the human residents.

The majority of country people had only a few simple furnishings: at most probably a bed or couch, a storage chest, a table, a bench or two, a cupboard, some large clay storage jars, and a hand mill for grinding grain. The kitchen area had a raised open hearth and, sometimes, an oven. To cook over the hearth fire, people would use a griddle, a spit for roasting meat (when it was available), and in some areas a cauldron hung on a tripod. In a small cottage, the hearth fire was the only source of heat. It also created a lot of smoke, which escaped through an open door or window, or through holes in the roof. Windows could be closed with wooden shutters, or may have been covered with oiled paper or a thin sheet of animal skin. The only artificial light came from oil lamps or, in areas that did not raise olives, candles made of beeswax or animal fat.

On most farms, there would be other buildings in addition to the house. The number and type of outbuildings depended on how well-off the family was and what they were raising. If the farm was prosperous, there could be a separate structure for the kitchen, a bathhouse, workshops for making olive oil and wine, storage buildings, and stables. Many such farms were arranged around a rectangular farmyard, with the house on one side and the additional buildings set along two other sides.

⌁ COUNTRY HOSPITALITY ⌁

On an everyday basis, most country people ate porridge, beans, occasionally a little pork, and probably some seasonal fruits and vegetables. The following passage from Ovid's long poem *Metamorphoses* describes a special-occasion meal (which would be easy to make today) and also gives several interesting details about how country people lived. In the selection, Baucis and Philemon, an elderly rural couple, are visited by two mysterious travelers. The old woman and man are poor, and they don't realize that their visitors are gods in disguise, but all the same they treat them with generous hospitality.

> So, when the gods came to this little cottage,
> Ducking their heads to enter, the old man
> Pulled out a rustic bench for them to rest on,
> As Baucis spread a homespun cover for it,
> And then she poked the ashes around a little,
> Still warm from last night's fire, and got them going . . .
>   . . . and then she took the cabbage
> Her man had brought from the well-watered garden,
> And stripped the outer leaves off. And Philemon
> Reached up, with a forked stick, for the side of bacon,

That hung below the smoky beam, and cut it,
Saved up so long, a fair-sized chunk, and dumped it
In the boiling water. They made conversation
To keep the time from being too long, and brought
A couch with willow frame and feet, and on it
They put a sedge-grass mattress. . . .
Baucis, her skirts tucked up, was setting the table
With trembling hands. One table-leg was wobbly;
A piece of shell fixed that. She scoured the table,
Made level now, with a handful of green mint,
Put on the olives, black or green, and cherries
Preserved in dregs of wine, endive and radish,
And cottage cheese, and eggs, turned over lightly
In the warm ash, with shells unbroken. The dishes
Of course, were earthenware . . .

                          . . . and the goblets
Were beech, the inside coated with yellow wax.
No time at all, and the warm food was ready,
And wine brought out, of no particular vintage,
And pretty soon they had to clear the table
For the second course; here there were nuts and figs
And dates and plums and apples in wide baskets—
Remember how apples smell?—and purple grapes
Fresh from the vines, and a white honeycomb
As centerpiece, and all around the table
Shone kindly faces, nothing mean or poor
Or skimpy in good will.

RURAL RETREATS

Although Horace once claimed, "In a poor cottage you may live a better life than kings and the friends of kings," his own country home was far from a cottage. Archaeologists have been exploring the site and the remains of Horace's villa for many years. Together with a large formal garden, it took up an area roughly the size of a football field. The entrance led directly into the garden, which had a pool at the center and was surrounded on all four sides by a covered walkway. At the back of the garden was the door into the house. The first room was an atrium, which would have been used as a living room and a place to welcome visitors. It was open to the sky, allowing in light and fresh air. Bedrooms were located off the atrium. More rooms, including a dining room, were arranged around a courtyard at the back of the villa. In addition, there was a private bathhouse that could be reached from the garden walkway.

An artist's re-creation of the inside of an upper-class Roman home. At the front is the atrium, with curtained entryways leading to other rooms on each side.

Horace's country home was considered quite a modest place in comparison with those of many rich people. The walls of Pliny the Younger's seaside villa, for instance, enclosed more than forty rooms and outdoor areas. These included an atrium; bedrooms for himself, his slaves, and guests; four dining rooms, each looking out on a different view; storage rooms for grain and wine; a ball court; an exercise area; a sunroom; a study; two courtyards; an herb garden; a large garden with a covered walkway and a small vineyard; and "a terrace fragrant with violets," as Pliny wrote to a friend in a letter that proudly and lovingly described his seaside retreat. He was trying to persuade this friend to come visit him, so along with portraying the villa's beautiful setting, he made sure to mention his home's conveniences:

Next comes the broad and spacious cold room of the baths. It contains two bathing tubs which project outward, from opposite walls, with curved rims; they are quite large, especially considering how close the sea is. Nearby are the room for applying bath oil, the furnace room, a corridor, and then two small rooms. . . . Adjacent to these is a marvelous warm pool from which swimmers look out over the sea.

Wealthy Romans appreciated their comforts, and they loved to be surrounded by art, especially in their country homes. Walls would be deco-

Young women exercising at a bathhouse

⁊ HOW TO SET UP YOUR VILLA ⓖ

Columella, who was born in Spain, wrote his book *On Agriculture* during the first century. In this work, Columella gave plenty of advice on how to run a large estate. Here are some selections:

The size of a villa or housing structure should be determined by the total area of the farm; and the villa should be divided into three sections: one section resembling a city home [for the landowner], one section like a real farmhouse [for the workers and livestock], and the third section for storing farm products. . . .

A household slave

Now in the farmhouse part of the villa there should be a large kitchen with a high ceiling . . . so that the wood beams may be secure against the danger of fire. . . . The best plan will be to construct the cells for unchained slaves facing south. For those in chains let there be an underground prison, as healthful as possible. . . . For livestock there should be, within the villa, stalls which are not subject to either cold or heat. For draft and pack animals there should be two sets of stalls, winter ones and summer ones. . . . Cells for oxherds and shepherds should be placed next to their animals so that running out to care for them may be convenient. . . .

The third part of the villa, that designated for storing produce, is divided into rooms for oil, for oil and wine presses, for aged wine, and for wine not yet fermented; into lofts for hay and straw; and into areas for warehouses and granaries. . . . the wine room is placed on the ground floor; but it should be far removed from the bathrooms, the oven, the manure pile, and other filthy areas giving off a foul stench. . . .

Now the following things ought to be near the villa: an oven and flour mill . . . ; at least two ponds, one for the use of geese and cattle, the other for soaking lupines, elms, twigs, branches, and other things which have been adapted to our needs. There should also be two manure pits, one to receive fresh dung and to keep it for a year, the other to provide old dung, ready to be carted off. . . .

It is also a good idea to enclose fruit trees and gardens with a fence and to plant them close to the villa, in a place to which all the manure seepage from the barnyard and the bathrooms can flow, as well as the watery dregs squeezed from the olives. For both vegetables and trees also thrive on fertilizers of this sort.

rated with richly colored frescoes of landscapes, mythological scenes, or decorative designs. The floors were ornamented with mosaics, some in black and white, others in many colors. The furniture was of the highest quality. When wealthy people ate, they reclined on cushioned dining couches—three set around a low table—often in their gardens. The gardens themselves were enhanced by statues, fountains, and shrubs trimmed into various shapes, such as animals, words, ships, and even hunting scenes.

The water supply for rich and poor country dwellers alike usually came from wells and nearby springs, streams, or rivers. The wealthy, of course, enjoyed luxuries that were not available to others—for example, the rich could cover their windows with sheets of transparent mica or, more rarely, glass. Some very prosperous people had an underfloor heating system called a hypocaust. Otherwise, they generally relied on charcoal braziers for extra heat in their many rooms. The charcoal smoldered smokily, and to feel the brazier's warmth a person had to be almost right next to it. In winter, therefore, the rich might be almost as cold as the poor. They also made do with the same limited sources of artificial light—although wealthy people had ornate lamp stands and candelabrums and could afford to use more oil and candles than poor people could.

IV

WORKING THE LAND

THE FARMER CLEAVES THE EARTH WITH SHARE AND CURVING PLOUGH.
THERE IS HIS YEARLY WORK: THAT MAKES FOOD
FOR HIS HOME AND LITTLE ONES,
FOR HIS CATTLE AND WELL-DESERVING OXEN.
—VIRGIL, *GEORGICS*

Wealthy landowners generally worked in the city in business and government. Rural property was an investment for them, a major source of wealth, but they very rarely took part in the actual work of the countryside. Of course, there were always a few landowners like Horace, who came to feel that he could only do his real work (writing poetry) in the peace of his farm. The poet wrote that he even enjoyed "digging and heaving rocks" from time to time. The future emperor Marcus Aurelius, too, thought that country chores could occasionally be fun. "We worked hard at picking grapes till we were covered with sweat and shouting with merriment," he said in a letter to his tutor, written from one of his family's estates. By and large, though, rural work was for the poor and unprivileged.

opposite:
A peasant or farm slave gathers up olives that have fallen to the ground.

181

SLAVE LABOR

Much of the labor on farms was done by slaves. Estate owners might have a great many; freeholders and tenant farmers, too, often had some slaves to help them with their work. Slavery was a fact of Roman life, as it was in most ancient civilizations. When the empire made new conquests, large numbers of war captives were enslaved. Slaves were also bought and sold in markets, many of which were located in Asia Minor. Children born to slaves automatically became slaves themselves. Sometimes referred to as "home-grown" slaves, they made up a large portion of the empire's enslaved population.

Uniquely for their time, the Romans very often freed their slaves. Freed slaves became Roman citizens, and their children could advance in society and even, occasionally, hold political office. Most rural slaves, however, did not enjoy such good fortune. Slaves who were freed were typically from the eastern part of the empire and worked in their owner's household, where he or she got to know them personally. Enslaved farm laborers, unless they were "home-grown," were generally from "barbarian" areas, such as Britain and Germany. Such slaves were unlikely to have a knowledge of Latin or Greek, or of the culture of the Mediterranean world. Moreover, they seldom came into contact with their masters. For these reasons, slaves who labored on large estates were almost never freed.

Farm slaves worked extremely hard, and they could be severely punished for any kind of disobedience. On some estates, owners kept unruly slaves chained together; they worked the fields as chain gangs during the day, and at night were locked in a prison. Pliny the Younger, however, assured one of his friends, "I myself never use chained slaves, nor does anyone else in this area." And Columella recommended that a master should personally make sure his slaves had decent food, clothing, and living conditions; should talk and even joke around with them; should allow them to complain about cruel treatment and then take action against it; and should reward especially

Captured Berbers, natives of North Africa, glumly wait to be sold as slaves.

good workers. All the same, many rural slaves endured very inhumane conditions. An example is found in this description of the often-beaten laborers at a flour mill, written by the second-century North African author Apuleius:

> Their skin was striped all over with livid scourge-scars; their wealed backs were crusted rather than clothed with their patchwork rags; some had no more covering than a bit of dangled apron; and every shirt was so tattered that the body was visible through the rents. Their brows were branded; their heads were half-shaved; irons clanked on their feet; their faces were sallow and ugly; the smoky gloom of the reeking overheated room had bleared and dulled their smarting eyes; and . . . their faces were wanly smeared with the dirty flour.

THE YEAR'S PATTERN

The realities of slave labor were far from the mind of Virgil when he wrote this loving description of a farm's seasonal cycle:

Without delay the year's yield burgeons out in fruit
or in young creatures or in nodding heads of grain,
loading the furrows with the crop, overflowing the bins.
Comes winter: then the generous olive yields its juice;
the pigs come home jolly with acorns; berries flourish.
Autumn too brings forth its various harvests; and high
upon the sunlit rocks the vintage ripens mellow.

Farm animals had to be fed and cared for year-round.

In fact, Virgil's poems about farming, the *Georgics,* never mention slavery at all. In his time and in the parts of Italy where he lived, small farms worked by free men were probably the norm. But although freeholders, tenant farmers, and sharecroppers did not suffer the cruelties of slavery, they still endured many hardships and long hours to raise their animals and produce their crops. There was always work to be done, whatever the weather and season.

Naturally the year's agricultural activities varied from place to place, depending on climate and environment. In Italy, the farming year began in March, when grapevines were pruned and wheat was sown. By May the grain plants were well established, and the furrows where they grew had to be weeded and hoed. This was also the month for shearing sheep and washing wool. And before the coming of summer's heat, conscientious farmers fertilized their fields and orchards with manure and compost.

June was the time for cutting grass to dry for hay, which farm animals would eat during the winter. In July farmers harvested barley and beans. In August the wheat was ripe, and it had to be harvested without delay, before the crop could be destroyed by birds, rodents, or storms. After harvesting, the grain had to be dried, then threshed to break the head of grain from the straw, then winnowed to finish cleaning the grain of seed coatings and other chaff. Threshing and winnowing could go on for months—these tasks were fitted in whenever there was a break from other farm chores.

September saw the ripening of various fruits, and preparations were made for the vintage, or grape harvest, which came in October. Some grapes were selected for eating fresh, but most were destined to be turned into wine. This was a lengthy process, which began with pressing the juice out of the grapes. They were placed on a raised floor in a press room, where barefoot workers trod on them. Grooves or channels in the floor allowed the juice to run out into containers. A mechanical press might be used to get the remaining juice out of the grape pulp. The grape juice then fermented in large jars, barrels, or vats, until the wine was ready. Some estates produced a tremendous amount

Pressing olives to make olive oil was hard work.

of wine—archaeologists estimate that on one three-hundred-acre estate in central Italy, more than 250,000 gallons were made a year.

In November, farmers planted winter wheat and barley. December was the month for fertilizing grapevines, planting beans, and cutting wood. Moreover, olives were now ripe and ready to pick. They had to be handled carefully. Varro explained, "Olives that can be reached from the ground or from ladders should be picked rather than shaken down, because fruit that has been struck loses flesh and yields less oil. . . . Those that are out of reach should be beaten down, but with a reed rather than a pole." Some olives were intended to be eaten, but most were pressed to make olive oil. Both the grape and olive harvests required many extra workers, so landowners or farm managers would hire local people or, in some parts of the empire, nomads to help out.

After all of this, farmers got a bit of a rest in January. They cut willow branches and reeds for basket making and other uses, repaired tools, and the like. Then in February it was time to start tending the grapevines and weeding the grain fields, getting them ready for the next planting.

OTHER OCCUPATIONS

While most people in the countryside worked at farming, rural areas also had some craftspeople, such as carpenters and blacksmiths; service workers, such as innkeepers and bakers; and what we would call professionals, particularly doctors and veterinarians. These people might be part of the labor force on a large estate, or they might live in a village and be available to anyone in the surrounding area.

A great many herders, in some parts of the empire, lived apart from village and estate life for much of the year. In spring they drove huge flocks of sheep or goats, or herds of cattle, up into mountain pastures, and there they stayed until autumn. This was a hard, lonely, and even dangerous existence. The herders followed their animals over steep and difficult terrain and were outdoors all day in all kinds of weather, with only little huts for shelter. As Varro wrote, "The type of man selected for this work should be strong, swift, agile and supple of limb; men who, as well as following the flock, can also defend it against wild beasts and robbers; men able to lift loads on to the backs of pack-animals, to dash out ahead, and to hurl javelins."

In coastal areas and around rivers and lakes, fishing was often more important than farming or herding. Some fishermen owned their own boats and equipment. Others might lease vessels and gear from someone else, in exchange for money or part of the catch. Seaside villas often included fish farms, with one or more tanks for breeding fish.

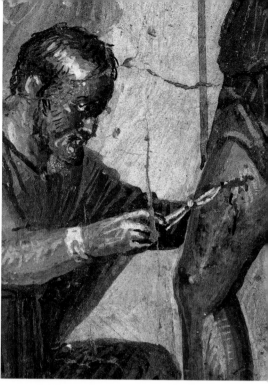

In this detail from a first-century fresco, a doctor concentrates on treating a man's injured leg.

Mining was the major activity in many rural districts. Most miners were slaves or convicts, and their lives were miserable. The historian Diodorus Siculus, toward the end of the first century B.C.E., wrote:

The slaves engaged in the operation of the mines . . . are physically destroyed, their bodies worn down from working in the mine shafts both day and night. Many die because of the excessive maltreatment they suffer. They are given no rest or break from their toil, but rather are forced by the whiplashes of the overseers to endure the most dreadful of hardships; thus do they wear out their lives in misery . . . although they often pray more for death than for life because of the magnitude of their suffering.

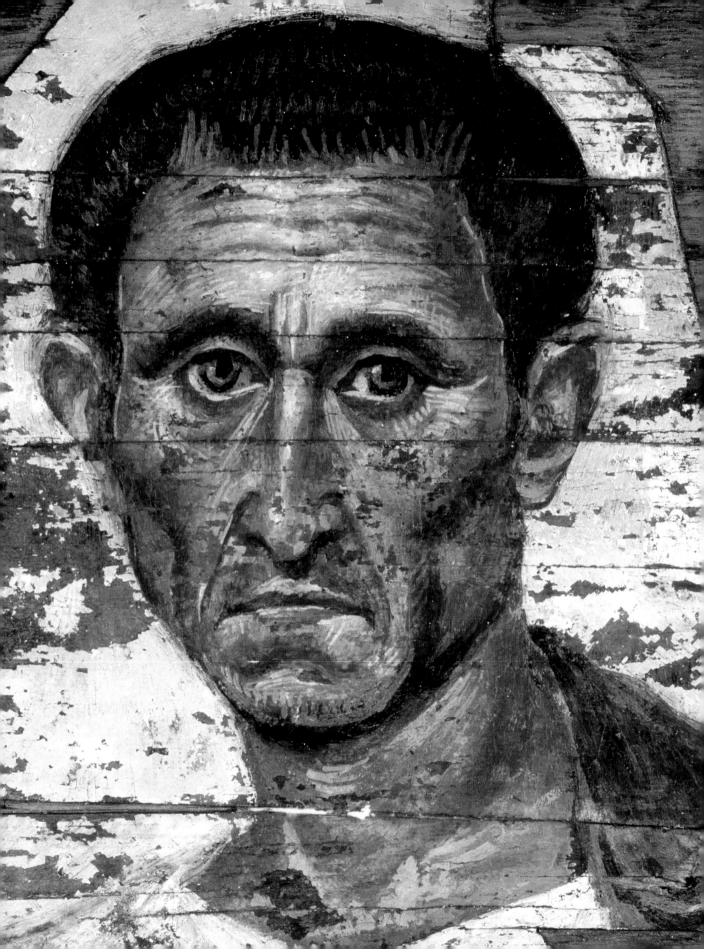

V

MEN OF THE SOIL

HAPPY IS THE MAN WHO REMAINS FAR FROM THE WORLD
OF BUSINESS, AS DID OUR PURITAN ANCESTORS,
AND WHO CULTIVATES THE FAMILY FARM WITH HIS OWN OXEN;
WHO REFRAINS FROM MONEYLENDING; WHO IS NOT A SOLDIER
ROUSED FROM SLEEP BY THE HARSH TRUMPET.
—HORACE, *EPODES*

In a Roman family, the father was the absolute head of the household. He was responsible for taking care of the family property and making all financial decisions. It was his duty to work hard and provide for his wife, children, and slaves. They, in turn, were expected to treat him with great respect and to always behave in a way that would honor him. But from the first century B.C.E. on, writers frequently complained that these old virtues were being neglected in the cities. In the country, on the other hand, the traditional values were said to be alive and well. It is hard for us now to tell whether or not that common opinion was true, for farmers and farmworkers almost never wrote about themselves. We can assume, however, that they did carry on with such Roman virtues as tough-

opposite:
A portrait of a Roman-Egyptian man, his face lined from care, hard work, and long hours in the sun

189

ness, perseverance, and hard work—not as an ideal, but because these qualities were necessary for survival.

LEISURELY LANDOWNERS

Generation after generation of Romans learned the story of Cincinnatus, a role model of ideal manhood. In 458 B.C.E., he was out plowing his fields when members of the Roman Senate came to beg him to take command of the army. Cincinnatus did not hesitate to do his duty, and he led the army to a swift victory. Sixteen days later, he resigned his command and returned to his little cottage, his fields, and his plowing. Recalling the stories of Cincinnatus and other farmer-heroes, Columella wrote in the first century C.E.,

> I am reminded by the great number of written records that our ancestors regarded attention to farming as a matter of pride. . . . I realize that the manners and strenuous lifestyle of bygone days are out of favour with present-day extravagance. . . . all of us who are heads of families have abandoned the sickle and the plough, and slunk inside the city.

Of course, Columella was thinking only of upper-class heads of families. But one reason that he wrote his book on agriculture was to convince some of these men that "one way of increasing one's fortune that is upright and above board . . . comes from cultivating the soil." He wanted landowners, even if they didn't work their estates with their own hands, to at least have a thorough knowledge of the principles of agriculture and farm management. That way they could appoint the right kind of men as bailiffs and foremen, they could make sound decisions about land usage and the like, and

A model of Pliny's seaside villa, clearly a place to relax and enjoy the good life

their estates would be as productive—and profitable—as possible.

Pliny the Younger was one landowner who took his responsibilities quite seriously. In a letter to a friend, he declared, "I am totally involved in farming," referring to his financial investments. He went on to ask the friend's advice about whether or not he should buy a certain piece of property. On another occasion, Pliny wrote to the emperor Trajan requesting a thirty-day leave of absence from his government duties so that he could go out to the countryside to settle some problems on one of his estates.

Several of Pliny's letters described not the responsibilities, but the pleasures of owning country property. He wrote of the leisure time he enjoyed when visiting his various villas. He slept as late as he wanted in the morning and lay about for a while thinking and then dictating letters or literary works to his secretary. A few hours later he went out and sat on the terrace to meditate and dictate some more. Then it was time for a carriage or horseback ride, followed by a nap. After that he might read aloud from a Greek or Latin speech. This would be followed by a walk, some exercise, and a bath. While he ate dinner with his wife and a few others, a slave often read a book to them. Then everyone would enjoy some music

ꙮ A FREEHOLDER'S LIFE: ꙮ
DAYDREAM VS. REALITY

Upper-class men were expected to lead useful lives serving the public, participating in politics and government, or managing vast business interests. So perhaps it is no wonder that upper-class poets often portrayed country life as an escape from reality. "Let another man heap up for himself the wealth of shining gold," wrote Tibullus. "May I be content to live on a little, . . . to avoid the summer's heat under the shade of a tree upon the bank of a flowing stream. And let me not think it shameful to hold a hoe once in a while."

This vision of a life of rural leisure contrasts sharply with an anonymous poet's realistic portrayal of a small freeholder's morning:

Simulus, the peasant farmer of a meager little plot, worried about gnawing hunger on this coming day. He slowly raised his weary limbs from his ugly little cot. With anxious hand he groped through the stagnant darkness and felt his way to the fireplace, burning his hand when he touched it. . . . With frequent huffs and puffs, he stirred up the sluggish fire. . . .

He unlocked the cupboard door with a key. Spread out on the cupboard floor was a paltry pile of grain. From this he took for himself as much as his measuring bucket held. He moved over to the mill and put his trusty lamp on a small shelf. . . . Then he slipped off his outer garment and, clad only in a shaggy goatskin, he swept the stones and inner portion of the mill. He put both his hands to work. . . . The grain which was ground by the rapid blows of the millstone poured out as flour. . . . At times he sang country songs and eased his labor with a rural tune. Or he shouted for Scybale. She was his only companion, an African woman. . . . He called her and told her to put firewood on the fireplace and to heat up some cold water. . . . [He mixed the flour with water and salt, formed a round loaf of bread, and put it to bake over the hearth fire. Then] hard-working Scybale plucked the bread out of the fireplace. Simulus happily took a piece in his hand. Now that he had put aside the fear of hunger and was free of anxiety, at least for this day, he tied leggings on his legs, covered his head with a leather cap, yoked his obedient oxen, drove them into the field, and sank his plow into the earth.

or a dramatic reading of a comedy. Before bed, Pliny took one more walk, along with some of his better-educated slaves, enjoying their conversation. This, he wrote, was his favorite routine, but sometimes it varied. He might join a hunting party (although he took writing materials with him, and usually worked on something literary while others pursued the quarry), or friends might drop by for a visit. And, of course, now and then he had to devote his attention to his tenant farmers and their complaints.

TENANT FARMERS

In one of his letters, Pliny told a friend that on some of his lands the tenants had gotten so far behind in paying their rents, they would never be able to catch up. Pliny decided that the best solution to this problem would be "to let out the farms on a share-cropping basis instead of a money rent, and then make some of my servants overseers to keep a watch on the harvest." These tenants were lucky that Pliny was willing to try a new arrangement with them. In many cases, when a tenant got behind in paying his rent, the landowner would seize and sell his equipment, slaves, livestock, and seed grain. This brought the tenant up-to-date on his rent in the short term— but he no longer had the resources to farm his holding.

Tenants on private estates typically leased their land for five years at a time. A wise landowner generally preferred to rent a holding to the same tenant over and over; the tenant would tend to think of the land almost as his own, and so would take better care of it. When he died, the lease might even pass to his son. The emperors came to encourage a similar stability on their estates. From the reign of Hadrian in the first part of the second century, an imperial tenant who brought new land into cultivation was guaranteed this land for the rest of his life. If he planted a fig orchard or vineyard, he could even have the land rent-free for five years; planting an olive orchard earned him ten years without rent.

Unlike wealthy landowners, tenant farmers and sharecroppers had very few opportunities for leisure. There were holidays, of course, when they did not work. Sometimes bad weather would give them a break from the heaviest outdoor chores. Then they might spend their time making baskets or nets, or mending tools. While engaged in such activities, they could also enjoy conversation and storytelling with family and friends. Now and then, a farmer might get away from his fields for a bit to go hunting or fishing. These could be relaxing activities, and if he was successful he would also have fresh meat or fish to bring home to his family. According to Virgil, who was probably thinking about the farmers of northern Italy, wintertime in particular brought opportunities for relaxation, enjoying company, and hunting:

> Winter's the tenant's rest.
> In the cold weather farmers mostly enjoy their gains,
> happily occupied in giving mutual parties.
> The genial winter's invitation frees from care. . . .
> But even so then is the time to gather acorns
> and bay-berries and olives and the blood-red myrtle;
> time to set snares for game-birds and nets for the stag
> and to pursue the long-eared hare; time to shoot deer,
> whirling the hempen thongs of a Balearic sling,
> when snow lies deep, when rivers hustle ice along.

VI

RURAL WOMEN

DELIA WILL GUARD THE HARVEST
IN HOT SUNSHINE UPON THE THRESHING-FLOOR;
OR SHE WILL SUPERVISE THE GRAPES HEAPING THE WINE-VATS
AND WATCH THE WHITE MUST* TRODDEN BY NIMBLE FEET. . . .
LET HER DIRECT THE WORK, AND GOVERN ALL THE WORKERS.
—TIBULLUS, *ELEGIES*

Under Roman law, free women did not enjoy the same status as free men. A woman nearly always had a male guardian—her father, husband, or another relative. In the case of a freedwoman, her guardian was generally her former master. The guardian was supposed to advise the woman on all her legal and financial dealings. Some guardians, however, gave their wards considerable freedom to make their own decisions. And a freeborn woman who bore three children was released from guardianship; four children earned a freedwoman the same privilege.

With or without guardians, though, women were still allowed to buy, sell, own, and inherit land. Pliny the Younger's letters give us two examples: in one, he offered to sell some of his lakefront property in

opposite:
Mosaic portrait of a young woman from southeastern Asia Minor

*grape pulp and skins

197

northern Italy to a woman friend. In another, he wrote to the manager of the farm that he had given to his old nurse, urging him to make the farm as profitable as possible so that the nurse would have a good living. Another example comes from a town in what is now Tunisia, where one of the area's major landowners in the second century was a woman named Valeria Atticilla. We also know that women owned luxurious seaside villas on the Bay of Naples, south of Rome.

WIVES AND MOTHERS

In Roman culture, a woman's main tasks in life were to marry, to care for her husband and his home, and to bear children to be his heirs. Fulfilling these roles, she was expected to uphold such traditional virtues as modesty, respectability, faithfulness, conscientiousness, and thriftiness. These Roman ideals spread to the upper classes throughout the empire. People living in rural communities in many provinces, however, often kept more to their own traditions. In some places, therefore, women had more rights and status than in Italy, but in other places they had less.

Although many babies in wealthy families were fed by wet nurses, most Roman women nursed their own children.

Girls married as young as eleven or twelve; by the age of thirty, a woman might well be a grandmother. A great many women, however, did not live that long. Childbirth was very difficult and dangerous in the ancient world. There were few medical techniques that could help a woman if something went wrong, and both mother and baby might well die. This tombstone inscription from what is now Hungary tells a common story:

> Here I lie, a matron named Veturia. . . . I lived for twenty-seven years, and I was married for sixteen years to the same man. After I gave birth to six children, only one of whom is still alive, I died. Titus Julius Fortunatus, a soldier of Legion II Adiutrix, provided this memorial for his wife, who was incomparable and showed outstanding devotion to him.

In memorials like this one, a husband often expressed his feelings for his dead wife, praising her virtues and the harmony of their marriage. Sometimes wives set up similar memorials for their husbands. Judging from these inscriptions and other sources, the ideal marriage was one where the couple lived together in peace, contentment, and mutual respect. Romantic love was perhaps not as important—since most marriages were arranged, the couple might not even know each other very well before their wedding. But often love grew. Once when Pliny the Younger's wife Calpurnia was staying in the countryside to recover from an illness, Pliny wrote to her from Rome, "It is incred-

A family portrait from an Italian villa

ible how much I miss you, because I love you and then because we are not used to being separated. And so I lie awake most of the night haunted by your image; and during the day, . . . my feet lead me, they really do, to your room; and then I turn and leave, sick at heart and sad."

HARD WORKERS

An upper-class woman did very little work other than supervising her slaves. Traditionally, though, women of every class spent much of their time spinning, weaving, and sewing. This was true of nearly all women in the countryside, as Tibullus poetically expressed it:

> The handiwork of dainty girls comes from the country—
>   the soft fleece grown by a pure white sheep:
> that is the work of women too, who turn the distaff
>   and whirl the spindle round with agile thumbs;
> meanwhile some busy indefatigable* weaver
>   sings, as the swinging loom-weights clash and ring.

Like rural women in most times and places, tenant farmers' wives probably did many farm chores. The bulk of their activity, though, likely involved preserving and preparing food, along with making cloth and clothing. Women slaves in the countryside did a variety of work, caring for farm animals and laboring in the fields, but Columella recommended that on cold or rainy days they instead do wool work. For slaves this would include cleaning and carding the wool as well as spinning it into thread.

Some female slaves accompanied shepherds up to the mountain pastures. These women, Varro explained, "can follow the flocks,

*tireless

200

prepare the shepherds' meals, and make the men more attentive to their work." He added that when he visited what is now Bosnia, he observed that the women there "are as good workers as the men . . . they can either do the shepherding, or bring logs for the fire and cook the food, or look after the farm implements [tools] in the huts."

The most important female slave on a large estate was the forewoman, who was the foreman's companion and assistant. (Usually they had a relationship like husband and wife, but slaves were not allowed to be legally married.) The forewoman's duties were wide-ranging. This selection from Columella's book covers just a portion of them:

While watching over her flock, a shepherdess also spins woolen thread using a distaff (in her left hand) and drop spindle.

> At one moment she will have to go to the loom and teach the weavers whatever she knows better than them. . . . At another moment, she will have to check on those slaves who are preparing the food for the *familia* [household]. Then she will also have to see that the kitchen, cowsheds, and even the stables are cleaned. And she will also have to open up the sick-rooms occasionally, even if they are empty of patients, and keep them free of dirt. . . . She will, in addition, have to be in attendance when the stewards of the pantry and cellar are weighing something, and also be present when the shepherds are milking in the stables. . . . But she will also certainly

⁊ BARBARIAN WOMEN ଽ

In some areas that the Romans conquered, women had a higher status than in the Mediterranean world. In fact, among the people whom Greeks and Romans referred to as barbarians, women could hold positions of great influence, even becoming political and religious leaders. Tacitus wrote that German warriors valued the praise of the women of their families more than any other praise. When injured, men went to their mothers and wives to have their wounds healed. According to tradition, sometimes when men were near to losing a battle, women's constant urging gave them the inspira-

The British queen Boudicca, as imagined by a nineteenth-century artist

tion and strength to win victory after all. "Moreover," Tacitus wrote, "they believe that within women there is a certain holiness and spirit of prophecy, and so the men do not scorn to ask their advice, nor do they ignore the women's answers."

The most famous British leader of Roman times was Boudicca, queen of the Iceni tribe in eastern Britain. In 61 C.E. she led a rebellion that nearly succeeded in driving the Romans out of Britain entirely. The historian Dio Cassius imagined her urging her warriors with words that voiced the anger many ruled by Rome must have felt:

You have learned by actual experience how different freedom is from slavery. Hence, even if anyone of you had previously . . . been deceived by the alluring promises of the Romans, . . . you have learned how great a mistake you made in preferring an imported despotism to your ancestral mode of life. . . . For what treatment is there of the most shameful or grievous sort that we have not suffered since these men made their appearance in Britain? Have we not been robbed entirely of our greatest possessions, while for those that remain we pay taxes? Besides pasturing and tilling for them . . . do we not pay a yearly tribute for our very bodies? . . . We have . . . been despised and trampled underfoot by men who know nothing else than how to secure gain.

need to be present when the sheep are sheared, and to examine the wool carefully.

A rural slave woman's other major duty was to give birth to children, who would be the property of the master—"home-grown" slaves were generally considered to be the best workers. Columella wrote that he rewarded slave women who bore several children. A woman who had three children was exempted from work (other than caring for the children, we assume). If she had four or more, she was given her freedom. The children, however, remained slaves.

VII
GROWING UP IN THE COUNTRYSIDE

FATHERS ORDER THEIR CHILDREN TO BE WOKEN UP TO DO THEIR
WORK EARLY. EVEN ON HOLIDAYS THEY DON'T ALLOW THEM TO BE
IDLE, AND THEY WRING SWEAT AND SOMETIMES TEARS FROM THEM.
BUT MOTHERS WANT TO HOLD THEIR CHILDREN ON THEIR LAPS AND
KEEP THEM IN THE COOL SHADE; THEY WANT THEM NEVER TO BE
MADE UNHAPPY, NEVER TO WEEP, AND NEVER TO BE IN DISTRESS.
—SENECA THE YOUNGER, *AN ESSAY ABOUT PROVIDENCE*

Like everything else in the Roman Empire, childhood experiences depended on many factors: whether you were rich or poor, free or slave, sickly or healthy; whether you lived in the country or the city; whether you were in the provinces or in Italy. Your mother might not live through childbirth, or she might die from complications during another pregnancy. Your father might be a good deal older than your mother and die while you were still a child. Or your parents could get divorced, in which case you would stay with your father. If your widowed or divorced parent remarried—

opposite:
A beautiful marble statue of a child hugging a young swan

which was common—then you would have a stepparent and probably stepbrothers and stepsisters. On top of everything else, you would be very fortunate simply to live through childhood: scholars estimate that nearly half of Roman children died before their tenth birthday.

COMING INTO THE WORLD

In the Roman Empire, nearly all babies were born at home. In the countryside, however, some hardworking women had their babies outdoors. Varro related that when he was traveling in what is now Bosnia, he saw that "pregnant women, when the time for delivery has arrived, often withdraw a short distance from where they are working, give birth there, and come back with the child you would think they had found, not borne." Afterward these women carried their babies around with them while they worked; Varro saw women nursing their babies even while they were hauling firewood.

Some babies, unfortunately, did not receive a joyful welcome.

Little babies, like this newborn being handed to its mother, were wrapped in swaddling clothes to keep them feeling warm and secure.

Because there was no reliable method of family planning, parents might already have more children than they could provide for. An extra mouth to feed could be a real burden. There were very few public assistance programs for families in this position, especially in the countryside; nor were there foster-care systems or adoption agencies. Some impoverished parents felt their only option was to expose, or abandon, their newborns, leaving them outdoors to either die or be picked up by a passerby.

This was a common practice throughout the ancient world.

It was the father's decision whether to raise a baby or expose it. Men were more likely to abandon daughters than sons, because it was felt that girls could not contribute as much to the family, and they would require dowries in order to get married. A mythological story retold by Ovid in his *Metamorphoses* was based on such a situation:

> Ligdus . . . was a poor man. . . . He told his pregnant wife . . . , "I pray for two things—that you may have an easy labor, and that you may bear a male child. For a daughter is too burdensome, and we just don't have the money. . . . I say this with great reluctance, so please forgive me—if you should bear a girl, we'll have to kill her."
>
> He spoke the words, and they both wept. . . . And Telethusa begged her husband over and over again to change his mind, but in vain. . . .
>
> She went into labor and gave birth to a girl. But the father didn't know this. And the mother lied, and raised her daughter as a boy.

A BRIEF CHILDHOOD

Upper-class children were largely cared for by slaves, often including a woman who nursed them. But most rural babies were breast-fed by their own mothers, probably for about two years. A peasant mother had little assistance with childcare, unless she had an older daughter who could help out.

Soon after children were toddling, they were probably given simple chores to do. Still, while they were quite young, they did have some playtime. Most rural children were likely to have few toys. On

A group of young
girls at play

the other hand, they would find plenty of things around the farmyard and fields to play with. A fallen branch could be a pretend sword; a large flower might make a beautiful, if not long-lasting, doll. A poem by Tibullus mentions country children building miniature cottages out of sticks. There was also plenty of room to run around in the fresh air, and we know that children enjoyed games similar to leapfrog, tag, and blindman's buff.

Various ball games were popular, too, including ones that resembled dodgeball, soccer, and field hockey. On a farm it was easy to find materials to make a ball. Some ancient types of balls were made of wool. Others were constructed from inflated pig bladders wrapped tightly in pigskin or leather. A ball that bounced fairly well could be made from cut-up sponges with string wound around them to make a sphere, all sewn into a cloth cover.

Young people then, as now, were often high-spirited. And if they happened to be rich kids on a visit to their country estates, they sometimes were not very considerate of the hardworking locals. Young men might be particularly rowdy and likely to disrupt peasants' routines. In the following passage, Marcus Aurelius—heir to the imperial throne and future philosopher—gleefully writes to his tutor about the trouble he caused for two shepherds and their flock:

When father was on the way home from the vineyards I jumped on my horse as I always do and set off down the road.

I hadn't gone far when I saw a large flock of sheep huddled together in the road as they do in places where the way is narrow. There were four dogs and two shepherds and nothing else. Then one of the shepherds, when he spotted our little gang riding up, shouted to the other one, "See them horsemen? They're the biggest robbers out!" When I heard this I dug my spurs into my horse and galloped straight into the sheep. They scattered in panic . . . baa-ing and bleating. One of the shepherds hurled his crook and it struck the man riding behind me. We beat it! The shepherd who was worried about losing his sheep broke his crook!

The older a child got, the more work he or she was expected to do, whether slave or free. Girls were taught wool working quite young. On estates, slave girls and boys looked after the sheep and goats that were kept on the farm. (Only grown men and women went with the flocks to distant pastures.) By the time they were ten or eleven, most rural children were working just as hard as the adults, and at almost as many tasks. The only things they really couldn't do yet were the jobs that took a lot of strength, such as plowing. But before many more years passed, they would be getting married and taking their full places in the adult world.

Nearly half of all Roman children died before they were ten years old. A grieving family had this statue placed on the lid of their child's sarcophagus, or stone coffin.

VIII

HARD TIMES AND HOLIDAYS

DRIVE DISEASES FAR AWAY. MAY MEN AND BEASTS BE HEALTHY. . . .
MAY I DRIVE HOME MY FLOCK AS NUMEROUS AS THEY WERE
AT DAYBREAK. . . . LET DIRE HUNGER NOT COME MY WAY.
LET THERE BE ABUNDANCE OF GRAIN.
—OVID, *CALENDAR*

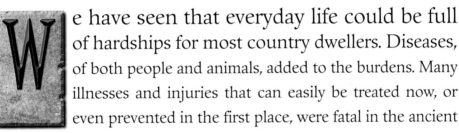

We have seen that everyday life could be full of hardships for most country dwellers. Diseases, of both people and animals, added to the burdens. Many illnesses and injuries that can easily be treated now, or even prevented in the first place, were fatal in the ancient world. There were not as many medicines available, and there was a less thorough knowledge of the workings of the human body and of surgical techniques. The possibility of crop failure also made famine a constant danger, and malnutrition was common.

A drought or other calamity could become even worse because of greed. For instance, in the late second century Galen, a doctor, wrote about what happened in one area that had suffered several years of bad harvests. The people of the town went out and "took from the

opposite:
Special events could give people of the Roman Empire a break from the hard work of their daily lives. These men are waiting at the finish line to honor the winner of a chariot race.

211

fields all the wheat, with the barley, beans and lentils." Because of this, the country dwellers had nothing to eat except "twigs and shoots of trees, bulbs and roots of unwholesome plants, and . . . wild vegetables." Nearly all the rural people developed diseases related to malnutrition, as well as conditions such as ulcers and tumors.

WAR AND PEACE

There was one hardship that most people in the Roman Empire were safe from during the first two centuries C.E. That was warfare, which in other times and places throughout history has taken a terrible toll on the countryside and its inhabitants. There were, of course, people who resented Roman rule and the military occupation of their lands, and sometimes these resentments flared up into rebellions. But most of the empire's residents seemed to agree with Tacitus when he wrote, "If the Romans are driven out—which Heaven forbid!—what will follow except universal war among all peoples?"

Thanks to Rome's strength, only communities near the empire's borders really had to worry about being attacked. This was the situation described by Ovid, living in exile on the west coast of the Black Sea, less than a hundred miles from the Danube frontier:

Countless tribes round about threaten cruel war, thinking it base to live if not by plunder. . . . When least expected, the foe swarms upon us like birds, and when scarce well seen is already driving off the booty. . . . Rare then is he who ventures to till the fields, for the wretch must plow with one hand, and hold arms in the other. The shepherd wears a helmet . . . and instead of a wolf the timorous ewes dread war.

CELEBRATING THE SEASONS

The weekend was unknown in the Roman Empire, although its Jewish population did observe a weekly day of rest. For others, every day was a workday—unless it was a holiday. Fortunately, there were many of these. On some of them, most work was forbidden by law—but farmers might feel that they had too much to do and could not afford to rest. Virgil wrote:

> Yes, even on holy days laws human and divine
> permit some work to be done. No ordinance forbids
> to irrigate the sown field or to fence it off,
> make ready snares for birds, burn up briers and thorns.

Slaves also had to work when others were relaxing and celebrating, although we know that some slaves, at least, were guaranteed a certain number of days off a year. When farmers did get to rest and enjoy a holiday, they liked to gather together family and friends—and often the laborers, too—for eating, drinking, and dancing. Country celebrations were usually outdoors, and in the summer people might build leafy bowers to provide extra shade. There might also be competitions, such as footraces, wrestling matches, and javelin-throwing contests. Nearly all Roman holidays had a religious significance, so prayers and ceremonies played a part in the day's activities, too.

Music and dance enlivened many celebrations. The man here is playing a double flute, while the woman not only dances but also plays castanet-like instruments.

A number of Roman festivals honored the events of the agricultural year. Naturally, these were particularly beloved celebrations in the countryside. Some of the most important were the Terminalia, the Parilia, the Robigalia, and the Ambarvalia.

The Terminalia occurred on February 23, when neighbors gathered at their *terminus,* the stone or post that marked the boundary between their lands. The head of each family placed on the *terminus* a small cake and a garland of flowers, and they set up an altar in front of it. Then, in the words of Ovid,

> Hither the farmer's country wife brings with her own hands on a sherd the fire which she has taken from her own warm hearth. The old man chops up wood. . . . Then he gets the kindling flames going with dry bark; his boy stands by holding the broad basket. After he has tossed corn [grain] three times into the fire his little daughter offers the pieces of honeycomb. Others hold out jars of wine; portions of each are cast into the flames. The company, dressed in white, look on in holy silence.

The Parilia arrived on April 21. This festival honored Pales, the goddess of shepherds. In the morning, shepherds or flock owners faced the east and repeated a prayer four times, asking the goddess to protect both people and animals. At the end of the prayers, the worshipper washed with the morning dew, then made an offering of mixed milk and wine. At the celebration's peak, sheep were driven through the smoke of a bonfire to purify them. Then, as the flames died down, shepherds took turns leaping over the fire.

On April 25 came the Robigalia, which often took place in a

grove of trees. This holiday's ceremonies were designed to keep rust and mildew away from the ripening grain. Ovid recorded a prayer to the god of rust, which included this appeal: "Put your hands on hard iron, not on tender crops. First destroy objects which can destroy others. . . . Let the hoes and the mattock and the curved plowshare, let all the farm equipment shine brightly, but let rust blemish weapons of war."

The Ambarvalia, at the end of May, was a day of purifying the fields and crops. No one was supposed to do any work, including the oxen who usually pulled the plow—they were left in their stalls, garlanded with flowers and given extra hay to eat. All those who wanted to take part in the ceremony were required to put on clean clothes and wash their hands in running water. Then they made a silent procession around the boundaries of the fields, leading a pig, a sheep, and an ox. Later there would be a feast, with music, singing, and dancing into the night.

The Romans developed early versions of many of our modern musical instruments. These men are playing a small organ and the ancestor of the French horn.

Life in the Roman Empire was hard, full of suffering for many and never-ending work for most. Yet there was much beauty, too, as poets and painters have shown us in their images of the countryside. Those who lived close to the land paid attention to its natural cycles and honored them with prayers and celebrations. The humblest farmer knew that a spring of pure water or a grove of trees was something special. The ancient Romans can inspire us, too, to take time now and then to remember the preciousness of nature and our rural areas, and to think gratefully of the many people who work so hard on farms around the world.

THE COUNTRYSIDE

RELIGION

I

A WORLD OF GODS AND SPIRITS

ROME IS A PLACE WORTHY OF THE PRESENCE OF ALL THE GODS.
—OVID, *FASTI*

The Roman Empire was a melting pot of religious attitudes and beliefs. Some people were passionately devoted to the gods; others probably went through the forms of religious ceremonies mainly for the sake of tradition. Many others stood between these two positions. People in the provinces often continued to worship as they had before their lands were conquered by Rome, but Roman religion also came to the provinces. Similarly, religious traditions from outside Italy made their way to Rome and became part of the Romans' belief system.

Religion was extremely important to the Roman state and to the Romans' sense of themselves. As the great orator and statesman Cicero wrote shortly before Augustus came to power, "If we com-

opposite:
Jupiter was the chief god of the Roman state and its special protector.

219

pare our history to that of other nations, we shall see that although we may be equal or inferior to them in other respects, we outshine them by far in religion, that is to say, in the worship of the gods." A centerpiece of Roman belief was the concept of *pax deorum,* "the peace of the gods"—the state of harmony and order that came with the proper relationship between humans and the deities. As long as the Roman people did their part to maintain *pax deorum,* it was believed, they and their empire would thrive. Gods and humans, after all, were members of the same community.

DIVINE POWERS

The Romans, like many peoples, felt that there was a kind of divine force or spirit present in every activity, in everything in the natural world, and even in the objects of daily life. This spirit was often called a *numen* (the plural form is *numina*). Awareness of the *numina* gave pious Romans the sense that the divine took part in all they did, wherever they went. For example, when they entered or left their homes, they were interacting with the *numen* of the threshold, Limentinus; when they swept the floor, the *numen* Deverra was present in the broom. A farmer tending his grain crop saw the powers of many *numina* at work, including Seia, the guardian of the seed while it was underground; Segetia, the spirit of the ripening grain aboveground; and Messor, the *numen* of harvesting.

Abstract ideas, too, had their *numina*. These were often personified as deities, usually goddesses, such as Fortuna (Luck), Pax (Peace), and Victoria (Victory). Similarly, the *numina* of provinces and cities were portrayed and honored as goddesses: for example, Britannia (Britain) and Roma (Rome). River spirits might be thought of as male or female: the Tiber River in Italy was watched over by the god Tiberinus, while the goddess Sequana was the personification of the Seine River in what is now France. As these examples show, there might not be a clear-cut difference between *numina* and deities. In general, we can say that all deities were *numina*—divine powers—but many *numina* were not imagined to take on human characteristics as gods or goddesses.

GUARDIANS OF HOME AND FAMILY

Every individual also had a *numen* or guardian spirit. This was known as a *genius* for a man and a *iuno* for a woman. The Genius Paterfamilias was the spirit of the father of the family, the head of the household. It was often symbolized as a snake. This *genius* protected not only the father, but also everyone else in the household, for whom the father was responsible.

Associated with the Genius Paterfamilias was the Lar, another kind of household guardian. Every family had its own particular Lar; some scholars think that the Lares (LAH-rays) were related to spirits of the family's ancestors. In artwork, Lares were often portrayed as dancing young men. They were so closely linked to the home that a Roman expression for "returning home" was *redire ad Larem suum:* "to go back to one's Lar." Along with the Lares, Roman families honored their household's Penates (pe-NAH-tays), guardians of the pantry or food cupboard. There were also public Penates, whose worship was related to the well-being of Rome, as well as Lares who were honored at crossroads in every district of the city.

This bronze statuette of a Lar stood in an honored place in a Roman home.

The hearth fire of each home was under the guardianship of the goddess Vesta, who was generally worshipped alongside the family Lares and Penates. Proper worship of Vesta was considered essential to the well-being of Rome. In her temple in the forum, the heart of the city, the goddess was symbolized by an eternal flame, which was tended by a group of priestesses called the Vestal Virgins.

THE GREAT GODS

While the Lares, Penates, and many *numina* had very specific areas of concern, the major deities looked after a wide range of interests. They were also felt to be particularly involved with the well-being of Rome and its empire. For this reason, they are often called the gods of the state religion. This was the official, formal religion of the empire and was full of time-honored traditions that maintained the relationship between the Romans and their gods.

Chief among the deities was Jupiter, known as the Best and Greatest. He was the chief protector of Rome, the giver of victory, and the guardian of emperors. In addition, like his Greek counterpart, Zeus, he was a god of the sky and the weather, especially thunderstorms. He also watched over agreements, contracts, and promises. Jupiter was often symbolized by an eagle.

Juno, the goddess who watched over women, childbirth, and marriage

Juno was the wife of Jupiter. She was particularly connected with women and marriage, but had other concerns as well. Like many Roman deities, she had a number of titles, which came from the various roles she played. Often she was called Juno Regina, "Juno the Queen." As Juno Lucina she was a goddess of light and of childbirth. She also had a military aspect and could be approached as Juno Curitis, "Juno of the Spear." Juno Sospita meant "Juno the Savior," referring to her role as a protector. Juno was closely identified with the Greek goddess Hera.

Minerva was mainly a goddess of crafts and warfare. As Minerva Medica, she was concerned with doctors and healing. In art she was generally shown wearing a helmet and might be holding a spear and shield, as was the corresponding Greek goddess, Athena.

Mars, often equated with the Greek Ares, is most familiar to us today as the Roman god of war. In the ancient world, however, he was also a protector of the crops and a god of springtime, when seeds were planted—this is why the month of March was named after him. Wolves and woodpeckers were sacred to Mars.

Venus, too, played various roles. We know her best as the goddess of love and beauty, like her Greek counterpart, Aphrodite. But Venus was also the *numen* of gardens, making them fertile to produce vegetables, fruit, and flowers. The Romans honored her as their divine ancestress, for she was the mother of Aeneas. This legendary hero, a refugee from the Trojan War, settled in Italy near the future site of Rome, and his descendant, Romulus, was said to have founded the city.

Mercurius, or Mercury, was the messenger of the gods. He was also a deity of abundance, trade, and success in business. Artists often portrayed Mercury in the same way as the Greek god Hermes, wearing winged shoes and a winged hat, carrying a staff with two snakes entwined around it (called a caduceus).

Other major Roman deities included Ceres, goddess of grain

Mercurius rests from a journey, his staff lying at his feet. An eighteenth-century English sculptor created this marble statue in the Roman style.

(equivalent to Greece's Demeter); Diana (Artemis), goddess of women, wild nature, hunting, and the moon; Apollo (whose name was the same in Greek), god of healing, prophecy, poetry, music, and the sun; Neptune (Poseidon), god of the sea and of horses; Hercules (Heracles), god of victory, strength, and business deals; Volcanus or Vulcan (Hephaestus to the Greeks), god of fire and metalworking; Pomona, goddess of fruit; Vertumnus, god of orchards and the changing seasons; Silvanus, a god of woodlands; and Castor, a god of horses, horsemen, athletes, and sailors. As can be seen, most of the deities of the state religion were felt to be quite similar to gods and goddesses from Greece. In fact, people in the eastern part of the empire usually worshipped the deities under their Greek names.

A mosaic of the sea god Neptune surrounded by fish

DIVINE HONORS FOR THE EMPEROR

Many peoples of the ancient Mediterranean world, including the Romans, did not draw a sharp line between the human and the divine. They recognized certain qualities as being godlike, and it was fairly easy to believe that people with those qualities could in fact become gods. The abilities to command armies, to win victories, to make laws, to govern peoples—these were all seen as having a kind of divine nature. It is not surprising, then, that the emperors, who wielded such powers, received divine honors.

The emperor Augustus was the adopted son of Julius Caesar, who was regarded as a god after his death. This made Augustus the son of a god, which increased his own authority. In some eastern provinces of the empire, where rulers had always been considered at least semidivine, Augustus and his successors were honored as gods not only after their deaths, but during their lifetimes as well. In Rome itself, however, Augustus refused to be worshipped. Instead, he encouraged people to honor his *genius*. Worshipping the emperor's guardian spirit quickly became an established and expected part of the state religion.

After Augustus died, he, like Julius Caesar, was officially deified (made a god)—as with Caesar, his achievements seemed superhuman. This was not the case with some of the succeeding emperors. In fact, the empire's third and fifth rulers, Gaius Caligula and Nero, were both egomaniacs who sought to be worshipped in Rome as gods during their lifetimes—for this and other reasons, both were hated by much of the Roman populace. The fourth emperor, Claudius, did better. He was deified after his death, for he had conquered Britain (something that even Caesar had not managed to do). By the last quarter of the first century, it was expected that all but the worst emperors would join the ranks of the gods after death. And so as the emperor Vespasian lay dying in 79 C.E., he was able to joke, "Alas, I suppose I am becoming a god."

PERSONAL SAVIORS

In addition to worshipping the great gods who ensured the well-being of the Roman people as a whole, individuals were often drawn to goddesses and gods who offered a more personal relationship. Many people were devoted to Aesculapius (in Greek, Asklepios), a god of healing. Worshippers in poor health might spend a night, or several nights, in his temple in the hope of receiving healing dreams from the god. These dreams could bring

The background of this relief shows a young man, assisted by a priest, going to sleep in the temple of Aesculapius. In the foreground, the god comes to the young man in a dream and heals his injured arm.

comfort, if nothing else. The orator and teacher Aelius Aristides had such an experience in a temple of Aesculapius in 146. He described "a feeling as of taking hold of him [the god] and of clearly perceiving that he himself had come, . . . and of hearing some things as in a dream, some waking; hair stood straight, tears flowed in joy; the burden of understanding seemed light."

Throughout the empire, the Egyptian goddess Isis inspired intense devotion. Many of her worshippers believed that all other goddesses were Isis under different names, playing different roles. Even under her own name, she was concerned with a great many things, among them love, childbirth, motherhood, healing, agriculture, weather, navigation, language, law, justice, war, and peace. Isis was a compassionate, merciful goddess who cared about the lives of those who prayed to her. Moreover, she could overrule the decrees of fate. She had restored her murdered husband, Osiris, to life, and so she also assured her followers a blessed afterlife.

Another deity who promised life after death was the god Bacchus. On one level, he was simply the god of wine, but in addition he represented freedom and ecstasy. He was identified with grapevines, which died back in winter and then came to life again in the spring. Cybele, or Magna Mater (meaning "The Great Mother"); Mithras, a god of light and truth; and the Greek earth goddesses Demeter and Persephone were also major deities who offered eternal life and the salvation or care of an individual's soul.

˜ ISIS, THE MOTHER OF ALL ⟆

The Golden Ass, a novel by the second-century author Apuleius, tells the story of a man named Lucius who meddles in magic that he doesn't understand. As a result, he is turned into a donkey, and in this shape he has many adventures and endures great suffering. At last, on the verge of despair, he sees the full moon rising over the sea and is inspired to pray for help. The goddess Isis appears to him in a dream and tells him how he can regain his human form. After he is restored to himself, he devotes the rest of his life to serving the goddess. Here is one of his prayers in praise of her, which expresses feelings shared by real-life worshippers of Isis:

Most holy and everlasting Redeemer of the human race, you munificently cherish our lives and bestow the consoling smiles of a Mother upon our tribulations. There is no day or night, not so much as the minutest fraction of time, that is not stuffed with the eternity of your mercy. You protect men on land and sea. You chase the storms of life and stretch out the hand of succour to the dejected. You can untwine the hopelessly tangled threads of the Fates. You can mitigate the tempests of Fortune and check the stars in the courses of their malice. The gods of heaven worship you. The gods of hell bow before you. You rotate the globe. You light the sun. You govern space. You trample hell. The stars move to your orders, the seasons return, the gods rejoice, the elements combine. At your nod the breezes blow, clouds collect, seeds sprout, blossoms increase. The birds that fly in the air, the beasts that roam on the hills, the serpents that hide in the earth, the monsters that swim in the ocean, tremble before your majesty.

·II·

BELIEFS AND CEREMONIES

AND WHAT REASON HAVE THE GODS FOR DOING DEEDS
OF KINDNESS? IT IS THEIR NATURE.
—SENECA THE YOUNGER, *MORAL LETTERS*

T he Roman state religion was practical, concerned with the here and now—the health, prosperity, and security of family, community, and empire. Religion and daily life were intertwined, and both were guided by the concept of *pietas*. The Romans understood this word to mean a proper sense of duty that encompassed all areas of life. *Pietas* involved conscientiously upholding correct, respectful relations with parents and other family members, ancestors, fellow citizens, government authorities—and deities. A person with *pietas* was careful to honor the gods by performing the traditional prayers and ceremonies of the state religion. These had clearly pleased the gods in the past, as the empire's strength proved, and so the established observances would continue to win divine favor for the Romans.

opposite:
An important part of many Roman religious rites was the offering of animals, such as this bull, in sacrifice to the gods.

229

The central part of most Roman religious rites was sacrifice. This was, literally, a sacred action, which involved making an offering to the gods. Because the deities gave so much to humans, it was considered only proper to give something back to them. The offerings could be fruit, flowers, wheat cakes or crackers, milk, wine, honey, or burning incense. They were often made on an altar before a statue of a goddess or god.

Major ceremonies generally called for "blood sacrifice," which would take place at an outdoor altar. Although this practice may be difficult to understand today, it was common in ancient times. In the Roman Empire, an animal would be chosen depending on the ceremony's purpose and the deity being honored. For example, a cow would be sacrificed to Juno, but a bull to Mars. The animal had to be perfect in health and appearance, and it could not struggle as it was led to the altar—an obviously unwilling victim was unac-

A sacrificial bull is held by two *victimarii*, the priestly assistants who will kill him as quickly and humanely as possible, while a flute player provides music for the ceremony.

ceptable to the gods. At the altar, a priest*
burned incense and made a libation, or liquid offering, of wine. Then he consecrated
the animal by sprinkling it with ground
and salted grain (called *mola salsa*), pouring
wine onto its head, and passing a knife
over its back. An assistant then killed the
animal; this was done swiftly, causing as
little pain as possible.

Sometimes the whole body was dedicated to the deity and burned on the altar,
but usually only certain parts were
burned. The rest of the animal either provided meat for a feast among the priests
and worshippers or was taken to be sold
in the marketplace. Describing the feast-
ing after a sacrifice, the author and philosopher Plutarch wrote,
"It's not the abundance of wine or the roasting of meat that makes
the joy of sharing a table in a temple, but the good hope and belief
that the god is present in his kindness and graciously accepts
what is offered."

Sacrifices were always accompanied by prayers. These had to
take a specific form, as the scholar Pliny the Elder explained:

A Pompeian
couple making
preparations for
a sacrifice.
The woman is
setting out
a *patera*, a
shallow bowl
used for pouring
libations.

It apparently does no good to offer a sacrifice or to consult
the gods with due ceremony unless you also speak words of
prayer. In addition, some words are appropriate for seeking
favorable omens, others for warding off evil, and still others
for securing help. We notice, for example, that our highest

*In many circumstances, government officials, army commanders, and
fathers of families could also function as priests and preside over sacrifices.

magistrates make appeals to the gods with specific and set prayers. And in order that no word be omitted or spoken out of turn, one attendant reads the prayer from a book, another is assigned to check it closely, a third is appointed to enforce silence. In addition, a flutist plays to block out any extraneous [distracting] sounds.

Roman prayers were very carefully worded. For example, if a farmer had to clear a woodland, he would want to make a sacrifice to the deity who watched over it—but he might not know for certain who that deity was. So his prayer would be phrased along these lines: "Whether you are a god or a goddess to whom this grove is sacred, as it is proper to sacrifice to you a pig as an offering to make up for disturbing this sacred place, whether I or someone I have appointed performs the sacrifice, I pray that you will show goodwill to me, my home, and my family." Prayers could also take the form of vows, in which the worshipper asked the deity to do something and promised to do something in return—usually to perform a sacrifice or set up an altar or statue to the goddess or god in question. Poorer people might give a small plaque or clay figurine to a temple in fulfillment of a vow.

In another kind of prayer (which scholars sometimes call a curse or hex), a person called on a deity to take action against a thief or other enemy. These prayers were often inscribed on sheets of lead and left in the temple of the god who was being appealed to. One example from southern Britain reads, "A memorandum to the god Mercury . . . from Saturnina a woman concerning the linen cloth she has lost. Let him who stole it not have rest before/unless/until he brings the aforesaid things to the temple, whether he is man or woman, slave or free."

❧ EVERYDAY MAGIC ❧

Almost everyone in the Roman world believed in magic. Most people did not disapprove of it, so long as it was not used to harm others. And sometimes what seems like magic or superstition was probably, to those involved, simply a way of praying or of being mindful of the role of the gods in their everyday lives. Or a "superstitious" practice might have been just a traditional custom whose religious meaning had long been forgotten. This passage from Pliny the Elder's *Natural History* shows how much religion, magic, and customary behaviors could overlap:

There is indeed nobody who does not fear to be spell-bound by imprecations [curses]. . . . On walls too are written prayers to avert fires. . . . The dictator Caesar, after one serious accident to his carriage, is said always, as soon as he was seated, to have been in the habit of repeating three times a formula or prayer for a safe journey, a thing we know that most people do today.

. . . Why on the first day of the year do we wish one another cheerfully a happy and prosperous New Year? . . . Why on mentioning the dead do we protest that their memory is not being attacked by us? Why do we believe that in all matters the odd numbers are more powerful. . . ? Why at the harvest of the fruits do we say: "These are old," and pray for the new ones to take their place? Why do we say "Good health" to those who sneeze? . . . Moreover, according to an accepted belief absent people can divine [know] by the ringing in their ears that they are the object of talk. . . .

We certainly have formulas to charm away hail, various diseases, and burns, some actually tested by experience, but I am very shy of quoting them, because of the widely different feelings they arouse. Wherefore everyone must form his own opinion about them as he pleases.

LEARNING THE WILL OF THE GODS

When Romans made a blood sacrifice, they generally wanted some sign that the deity had accepted the sacrifice and looked favorably on the worshipper. For this reason, men known as *haruspices* were called on to examine the animal's internal organs. A *haruspex* knew the normal shape, color, and condition of the organs. If there were deformities or other differences from what was normal, the *haruspex* understood what these symbolized. The Romans believed that the gods "imprinted" the marks of their favor or disfavor on the organs as the animal was being consecrated. If the signs showed that the sacrifice was unacceptable, a further sacrifice would have to be made.

Before a person took any major action, it was important to find out if the gods approved. This was another occasion when a *haruspex* might be called on to examine the organs of a sacrificed animal. In this case, if the signs were unfavorable, the person could abandon the project, wait until the signs were better, find some way to earn the gods' favor—or go ahead as planned and risk divine displeasure. But most Romans knew plenty of stories about what could happen to people who took these risks, such as generals who ignored the gods' warnings and suffered dreadful defeats.

Another way of learning whether the gods approved of an action or not was augury. This was also known as "taking the auspices." Augury generally involved marking out a particular area, in the sky or on the ground, and then watching and interpreting the behavior of birds in that area, especially eagles, vultures, and crows or ravens. The priests who explained what the birds' flight patterns and eating habits meant were called augurs. They were

Worshippers in Roman-ruled Egypt hold a riverside ceremony to seek the goodwill of the gods of the Nile.

also responsible for marking out various kinds of sacred boundaries, such as the places where temples would be built.

The deities could send warnings without being asked for them—sometimes through bolts of lightning, at other times through "prodigies." In general, prodigies were unusual happenings in the natural world, or they involved something being very out of place, such as a wild animal showing up within a city. *Haruspices* explained the meaning of lightning flashes and prodigies and recommended the proper actions to take in order to prevent the harm that was warned against. For example, when a horned owl—considered a very unlucky bird—was found in a temple in Rome in 43 C.E., the whole city had to be purified and protected with sacrifices, prayers, and a solemn procession around the *pomerium,* or sacred boundary line.

INITIATIONS

For a great many Romans, this world was the only one with which they concerned themselves. They either did not believe in an afterlife or did not worry themselves about it. Residents of the empire

This fresco from Herculaneum, Italy, shows initiates of the Mysteries of Isis taking part in a ceremony in honor of their goddess.

who were drawn to the worship of deities such as Isis and Bacchus, on the other hand, were a good deal more interested in the world beyond this one. These worshippers did not reject the state religion, but alongside it they wanted a spiritual path that had a greater mystical, emotional, and personal feeling.

These "in-depth" spiritual practices have come to be known as the Mysteries, or mystery religions. The term comes from the Greek *mystes,* "an initiate." Initiates were people who went through a ceremony that brought them closer to a particular goddess or god, deepened their understanding of the spiritual dimension of life, and gave them a promise of overcoming death. The ceremonies were kept secret from outsiders, and in any case were difficult to describe in words. These experiences were highly symbolic, and only someone who had been through them would really understand the meaning of them. In general, however, we can tell that initiations usually included purification, spiritual ordeals or trials, beholding sacred symbols, hearing sacred chants or stories about the deity, and a symbolic death and rebirth. This is how the second-century orator and novelist Apuleius described initiation into the Mysteries of Isis:

> I approached the confines of death. I trod the threshold of Proserpine [the goddess of the underworld]; and borne through the elements I returned. At midnight I saw the Sun shining in all his glory. I approached the gods below and the gods above, and I stood beside them, and I worshipped them. Behold, I have told my experience, and yet what you hear can mean nothing to you.

·III·

SACRED
PLACES

WE HAVE A CITY FOUNDED BY THE AUSPICES AND AUGURY;
THERE IS NOT A CORNER OF IT THAT IS NOT FULL OF . . . OUR GODS.
—LIVY, *AB URBE CONDITA*

Places were important in Roman religion. Rome itself was in many ways considered a sacred site, chosen by deities and heroes long ago as a place of greatness. One sign of the city's religious character was the *pomerium* that enclosed it. This boundary was a strip of land that set off the city as a sacred place. It was marked at every change of direction by six-foot-tall blocks of stone. Any emperor who enlarged the empire was allowed to also enlarge the *pomerium,* and this was done on several occasions. When the Romans founded a colony,* its *pomerium* was laid out just like Rome's. After the auspices were taken, the founder of the colony ceremonially plowed a furrow around the location. This procedure showed that colonies were intended to be "little Romes" where, among other things, the

opposite:
Many of Rome's sacred places no longer exist or are in ruins. Some, like this temple (shown in a twentieth-century painting), survived because they were later turned into Christian churches.

*A Roman colony was a settlement in Italy or the provinces for retiring soldiers and other citizens.

Roman deities would be honored. Whether in the capital or the colonies, burials were not allowed within the *pomerium,* for they would contaminate the holy ground.

HOUSES OF THE GODS

In his great epic *The Aeneid,* the poet Virgil included an episode in which the hero, Aeneas, is shown important landmarks of what will someday be the city of Rome. Among the sights is a hill covered with tangled thickets. Despite its wild and uninviting aspect, Aeneas is aware of the "god-haunted feel of the place." His guide tells him,

> In this grove, on this hill with leafy summit, there lives
> A god—but which god, we can't be certain. Yet some believe
> They've seen Jupiter himself, have often seen him brandish
> In his hand his dark shield when he stirs up the clouds.

The gods of Rome's Capitol, with their sacred birds sitting beside their right feet: an owl for Minerva (far left), an eagle for Jupiter (unfortunately, everything but its talons and part of a wing have broken off), and a pea-cock for Juno

After Rome was founded, this hill became the location of the Capitol, the great temple of Jupiter, Juno, and Minerva, together known as the Capitoline Triad. Many cities throughout the empire also came to have Capitols, dedicated to the same three deities. A Capitol was nearly always built on a hill or rise, generally close to the city's forum, or political center.

Inside the Capitol were statues of each member of the Triad. Each statue stood in its own *cella,* or "room." Most temples, however, were dedicated to only one deity and so had only one *cella.* Classical Roman temples were rectangular in shape and elevated on a high platform called a podium, which might have storage areas beneath it. At the front of the temple a wide stairway led from the ground to the top of the podium. Here there was a columned porch, sometimes taking up as much as half the temple's length. The *cella,* enclosed by solid walls at the back and sides, was behind the porch.

The architect Vitruvius, writing during the reign of Augustus, recommended that, whenever possible, temples and statues face west:

> This will enable those who approach the altar with offerings or sacrifices to face the direction of the sunrise in facing the statue in the temple, and thus those who are undertaking vows look toward the quarter from which the sun comes forth, and likewise the statues themselves appear to be coming forth out of the east to look upon them as they pray and sacrifice.

A few Roman temples were circular. The temple of Vesta was built in this shape because it was intended to resemble the round huts in which the earliest Romans lived. Hercules also had a small, circular temple in Rome. A much grander building, though, was the

CEREMONIES FOR REBUILDING A TEMPLE

In 69 C.E. Rome's Capitol was destroyed in a fire. The next year, the emperor Vespasian had this important temple rebuilt. The historian Tacitus described the ceremonies that began the reconstruction:

On June 21, beneath a cloudless sky, the entire space devoted to the sacred precinct was encircled with fillets [ribbons] and garlands. Soldiers who had auspicious names entered with boughs of good-omened trees. Next, the Vestal Virgins, together with boys and girls both of whose parents were alive, sprinkled it with water drawn from springs and rivers. Then the praetor [city official] Helvidius Priscus, in terms dictated by the pontiff [priest] Plautius Aelianus, having first purified the area with pig-sheep-bull sacrifices and placed the entrails on an altar of turf, prayed to Jupiter, Juno, and Minerva, and to the tutelary gods of the Empire, to prosper the undertaking and by their divine help to raise up their abodes begun by human piety. He then touched the fillets which were wound around the foundation stone and entwined around the ropes. At the same time the other magistrates, the priest, senators, *equites,* and a great part of the people, uniting their efforts with zeal and joy, dragged the huge stone. Everywhere there were thrown into the foundations contributions of silver and gold, and of virgin metals never smelted in furnaces but in their natural state; the soothsayers had previously declared that the work should not be defiled by stone or gold intended for any other purpose. The height of the temple was increased; this was the only variation which religious scruple permitted, and the one feature which had been thought wanting in the magnificence of the old temple.

The inside of a round Roman temple that has been converted into a church, drawn by an Italian artist around 1800

Pantheon, a temple like no other. Behind its porch was a huge rotunda, roofed with a spectacular dome. In the center of the dome was a wide circular opening to let in sunlight. The lofty dome was probably intended to represent the sky, with the opening symbolizing the sun. Some of the deities worshipped in the Pantheon may have been those after whom the planets were named—we know that Venus and Mars, for example, were honored there.

ALTARS

Temples of the Roman state religion were not meant to hold groups of worshippers. An individual could go into a temple to honor the deity privately, burning incense or leaving an offering on a small altar before the statue of the goddess or god. Public, group worship took place outside the temple, focusing on an altar erected at the foot of the stairs. This was where all blood sacrifices performed at the temple took place. (Blood sacrifices had to be conducted outdoors, under the open sky.) Only the priest spoke during the ceremony; everyone else participated with their minds and hearts, but not with their voices.

All temples had altars, but altars did not need to be at temples.

Families had small altars in their homes and, quite often, outdoor altars on their property for blood sacrifices. Travelers sometimes set up roadside altars to thank a deity for protection on a journey. Some altars were part of open-air shrines, such as those dedicated to the Lares at crossroads in Rome. Small public altars were used for incense and other bloodless offerings.

Two very important altars—used for blood sacrifices—were the Ara Pacis, the "Altar of Peace," and the Ara Maxima, the "Greatest Altar." Both were located in Rome. The Ara Pacis was an impressive monument, dedicated by the emperor Augustus in 9 B.C.E. Made of marble, it was U-shaped and surrounded with a nearly square wall, twenty-three feet high, that had openings on the east and west sides. A low podium supported this whole complex. Both altar and wall were adorned with wonderful sculptured reliefs that included images

The Ara Pacis has been reconstructed near its original site. This is the front entrance; the stairs lead up to the actual altar. On the upper right of the wall, the hero Aeneas is shown preparing to make a sacrifice.

of Mother Earth, the emperor and his family, an episode from the story of Aeneas, and other legendary and ceremonial scenes.

The Ara Maxima was probably called the "Greatest" because of its ancientness. It was dedicated to Hercules, who was said to have set it up himself, making the first sacrifice at it. This altar was a place where businessmen often met to agree on deals, and where merchants sometimes came to pledge a tenth of their profits to Hercules. Women were not allowed to approach the Ara Maxima because, according to one legend, a priestess of Bona Dea (the Good Goddess) once refused to give Hercules a drink of water from the goddess's sacred spring.

THE DIVINE IN NATURE

Many places and objects in the natural world had a religious significance. Sources of rivers, hot springs, groves of trees, and the like were felt to be holy places, where divine powers were strongly present. Worshippers might set up shrines or altars to deities on these sites, or there could even be full-blown temples. For example, we know of a few temples that were located in sacred groves outside of Rome. Most famous was the sanctuary of Diana in the wood of Nemi. The temple was built beside a small lake inside the grove, about sixteen miles from Rome. Archaeologists have found numerous clay figurines at the site, left as offerings by grateful worshippers.

Another much-loved sacred site was the source of the Clitumnus River, a tributary of the Tiber. The author-senator Pliny the Younger has left us this description:

There is a fair-sized hill, dark with ancient cypress-woods. Beneath this the spring rises, gushing out in several veins of

The emperor Hadrian had this statue of a river god set up on the grounds of his villa, or country retreat.

unequal size. After the initial flow has smoothed out, it spreads into a broad pool, pure and clear as glass, so that you can count the coins that have been thrown into it. . . . Near it there is an ancient and venerable temple. In it stands [an image of] Clitumnus himself, clothed, and draped in a crimson-bordered robe. . . . Around this temple there are several smaller shrines, each with its god. Every one has its own cult [worship dedicated to it], its own name, and some even their own springs.

The Romans firmly believed that every place had a guardian spirit, its *genius loci,* "the spirit of the place." Sometimes, as with Clitumnus, the name of the *genius* was known; sometimes it was not. Either way, the Romans believed that these powers should be honored. Many soldiers stationed at outposts in the provinces seem to have been particularly careful to honor such spirits. Archaeologists have found a number of altars dedicated to the "*genius* of this place" at forts on the empire's frontiers. But with or without temples, altars, shrines, or statues, the presence of the divine in nature remained clear to many Romans. The philosopher-statesman Seneca the Younger eloquently expressed this feeling in a letter to one of his friends:

> If you have ever come on a dense wood of ancient trees that have risen to an exceptional height, shutting out all sight of the sky with one thick screen of branches upon another, the loftiness of the forest, the seclusion of the spot, your sense of wonderment at finding so deep and unbroken a gloom out of doors, will persuade you of the presence of a deity. Any cave in which the rocks have been eroded deep into the mountain resting on it, its hollowing out into a cavern of impressive extent not produced by the labours of men but the result of the processes of nature, will strike into your soul some inkling of the divine.

·IV·
RELIGIOUS ROLES FOR MEN

EACH HOUR BE MINDED, VALIANTLY AS BECOMES A ROMAN
AND A MAN, TO DO WHAT IS TO YOUR HAND, WITH . . .
UNAFFECTED DIGNITY, NATURAL LOVE, FREEDOM, AND JUSTICE. . . .
YOU SEE HOW FEW THINGS A MAN NEED MASTER IN ORDER
TO LIVE A SMOOTH AND GODFEARING LIFE.
—MARCUS AURELIUS, *MEDITATIONS*

The model of Roman manhood was Aeneas. In Virgil's *Aeneid,* the hero is frequently called *pius* Aeneas because of his supreme devotion to duty. A favorite subject in Roman art was Aeneas carrying his weak and aged father away from the conquered city of Troy. Aeneas's *pietas* toward his father was only surpassed by his *pietas* toward Jupiter, the father of the gods. At every turn, the hero followed the god's will, even when it caused him great personal unhappiness. Having fled the destruction of the Trojan War, he knew that his duty was to follow Jupiter's guidance and find a new home for himself and all who depended on him.

opposite: **Aeneas carries his father away from war-torn Troy. The great seventeenth-century sculptor Bernini created this beautiful statue.**

Aeneas's fatherly concern for his people mirrored the fatherliness of Jupiter. Fatherliness, in fact, was one of the most valued qualities in ancient Rome. It was expected especially from leaders, whether in the government, the army, the local community, or the family. And whether a man was *pater patriae,* the "father of the country" (ruler of the empire), or *pater familias,* the "father of a family" (head of the household), he had the responsibility of ensuring that everyone who depended on him would enjoy the peace of the gods.

A FATHER'S DUTIES

Home-based worship was a very important part of Roman religion. It was a father's duty to lead this worship, acting as a priest for his entire household, including slaves as well as family members. He was responsible for maintaining a *lararium,* the family shrine to the Lares. This could be a freestanding shrine, a wall niche, or even a painting on the wall. In well-to-do homes, it was generally located in the garden, kitchen, or atrium, which was something like a modern living room. Some men, including the emperor Augustus, also had a *lararium* in their bedroom. One of the first things a *pater familias* did after getting up in the morning was light incense at the *lararium,* and he might worship the Lares in this way again at bedtime.

At dinnertime, the family honored the Lares, Penates, and the goddess Vesta. Traditionally, the whole household gathered in front of the *lararium* to call on the deities before going to the table. After the appetizer course, the family was silent while the father made an offering by throwing *mola salsa* and a choice piece of meat into the hearth fire or a small altar fire. These ancient customs were cherished by many Romans. The poet Horace, for example,

This wall-niche *lararium* from Pompeii shows the father of the family with a Lar dancing on each side of him. The snake symbolizes the father's *genius*, or guardian spirit.

wrote, "O, divine nights and meals where we eat, my family and I, before the Lar of my own home."

The *pater familias* was also responsible for maintaining a proper relationship between his family and the dead. In the *lararium,* or in another special place, he kept busts or wax masks of his ancestors. During the festival of Lemuria (May 9, 11, and 13), he had to make sure that unhappy ghosts would not harm the living. Each of the three nights, when everyone else was asleep, the *pater familias* got up, made a gesture against evil, and washed his hands. Then, barefoot, he walked through the house with nine black beans, food for the dead because beans were believed to contain a kind of life force of their own. He threw them back over his shoulder one at a time, proclaiming, "With these beans I redeem both myself and my household." When his task was done, this

~A LANDOWNER'S *PIETAS*~ .

In North Africa around 156 C.E., Apuleius was accused of having used magic to get a wealthy widow to marry him. In his successful defense speech, he portrayed himself as a properly religious man. He pointed out that the prosecutor, on the other hand, was notable for his lack of *pietas* and neglected his duty to the spirits that inhabited the land he owned:

> Even to the rural deities who give him food and clothing he never once offers the first-fruits of his crops, his vines or his herds. On his lands there is not a single sanctuary or holy site or wood! And why mention groves or chapels? Those who have been at his place declare they have never seen so much as a stone anointed with oil or a branch adorned with a garland anywhere on his estate.

In contrast, here is a passage from the poet Martial (ca. 40–ca. 104), who has regretfully sold his farm and asks the buyer to honor the gods there as he has done:

> I entrust to your care these twin pine trees, the glory of their untilled grove, and these holm oaks, haunted by fauns [woodland spirits], and the altars of Jupiter, the thunder god, and shaggy Silvanus which my unlettered farm manager built with his own hands. . . . I also entrust to your care the virgin goddess [Diana] of the sacred sanctuary and Mars, who ushers in my year . . . , and also the laurel grove of tender Flora. . . . Whether you propitiate all the kindly deities of my tiny little farm with a blood sacrifice or incense, please tell them this: "Wherever your Martial is, though absent, he is yet in spirit a suppliant with me, making this sacrifice to you. Consider him to be present and grant to each of us whatever we may pray for."

pious father could feel some assurance that the dead were satisfied and would not carry off any of his family to join them in the
underworld.

PRIESTS OF THE STATE

As it was a father's duty to maintain the *pax deorum* for his family,
other men took this responsibility on behalf of the state as a whole.
First and foremost in this role was the emperor himself. He was the
pontifex maximus, the chief priest and head of the state religion. All
other priests in the city were appointed by the emperor, and they
held their positions for life. These men were wealthy, educated senators, whose religious duties were only part-time. About
one-quarter to one-third of Roman senators served as priests. This
mix of priesthood and politics may seem odd to us, but it made perfect sense to the Romans. As Cicero explained:

> Among the many things . . . that our ancestors created and
> established under divine inspiration, nothing is more
> renowned than their decision to entrust the worship of the
> gods and the highest interests of the state to the same men—
> so that the most eminent and illustrious citizens might
> ensure the maintenance of religion by the proper adminis-
> tration of the state, and the maintenance of the state by the
> prudent interpretation of religion.

The city of Rome had sixteen priests called pontiffs (in Latin,
pontifices). They oversaw such matters as adoptions, wills, and burials. Traditionally, they were also in charge of the calendar (setting
the dates of movable holidays, for example) and of record keeping

A priest preparing for the sacrifice of a pig. At sacrifices, Roman priests covered their heads so that they would be less likely to see or hear anything unlucky that might mar the ceremony.

for the city. Mainly, though, they were experts in religious law. They made sure that government officials who had religious duties performed them properly, and also oversaw "all the priesthoods" and their helpers "to make sure that they commit no error in regard to the sacred laws," as the historian Dionysius of Helicarnassus wrote. He added, "For private citizens who are not knowledgeable about religious matters concerning the gods and divine spirits, the *pontifices* are explainers and interpreters." Rome's pontiffs could exercise authority in nearby towns and cities, but not in the provinces. Roman colonies had their own pontiffs as well as augurs.

Fifteen priests known as flamens also belonged to the college, or association, of pontiffs. Each flamen served one particular deity. Most important was the Flamen Dialis, the priest of Jupiter. Unlike the other flamens, he had to follow a number of ancient rules. For example, he could not touch a dead body, he could not be absent from Rome for longer than several days at a time, and he had to have been married only once and in the most formal type of wedding ceremony. His wife, the Flaminica Dialis, assisted him in some of his duties and had to follow the same rules. Other Italian towns, as well as Roman colonies, also had flamens. In addition, priests who looked after the worship of the deified emperors, both in Rome and the provinces, were called flamens.

The augurs formed another major priestly college. They interpreted the will of the gods and laid out sacred space. The college had sixteen members, one of whom was the emperor. There were several other priesthoods in Rome. Among them was the twelve-member Arval Brotherhood, which performed regular sacrifices for the health of the emperor and his family. The Salii were twenty-four priests of Mars, famous for the leaping dances they performed at certain festivals in the god's honor.

Most priests of the state religion were not assigned to serve in any particular temple. Each temple, however, had its own custodian living next to it. If an individual wanted to make a sacrifice at the temple, the

The god Mars, who was served by the Flamen Martialis

custodian was the one who would arrange it. In addition, he was in charge of looking after the building and had a staff of servants and slaves to do the actual work of keeping the temple clean and in good repair. Many temples also had gatekeepers, clerks, guides for visitors, and other workers.

FOR MEN ONLY

Many men were drawn to the mystery religions. Some were initiated into the Mysteries of Demeter and Persephone, others became priests of Cybele, and still others, like Apuleius, devoted themselves to Isis. But perhaps the most popular mystery religion for men was that of Mithras. In fact, only men were allowed to become initiates of Mithras. The god was particularly attractive to soldiers, who carried Mithraism (along with traditional Roman religion) throughout the empire.

A priest of the goddess Cybele, shown with cymbals and other objects used in her worship

Although Mithras was originally a Persian god, his worship in the Roman Empire took on its own unique form. Its ceremonies were secret, but literature and archaeology have revealed some information. Group worship took place in caves or small, cavelike rooms. A bull sacrifice played a major role, since Mithras had slain a great bull in order to give life to the earth. There were also rites of purification and ceremonial meals of bread and water, or perhaps wine mixed with water. Initiates of Mithras progressed through seven ranks, known as Raven, Bridegroom, Soldier, Lion, Persian, Sun Runner, and Father. Each of these was associated with a planet, and astrology seems to have played some role in Mithraism. But as with the other mystery religions (and even with some aspects of Rome's state religion), it is almost impossible for scholars today to know or understand many details of the worshippers' beliefs and practices.

This second-century statue from Rome's port city, Ostia, shows Mithras slaying the great bull.

V

WOMEN AND WORSHIP

WOMEN [ARE] THE CHIEF FOUNDERS OF RELIGION. . . . WOMEN . . .
PROVOKE MEN TO THE MORE ATTENTIVE WORSHIP OF THE GODS,
TO FESTIVALS AND TO SUPPLICATIONS.
— STRABO, *GEOGRAPHY*

When we want to study women's experiences in the Roman world, we run into a very large problem: almost nothing written by any Roman woman has survived to the present.

In general, male authors were not interested in describing many aspects of women's lives, especially their thoughts and feelings. Men often looked down on women, and wrote about them mainly to criticize or make fun of them. Roman law actually placed most women in the same legal position as children. With few exceptions, women were required to have male guardians throughout their lives. In the area of religion, writers often painted women's beliefs and practices as being irrational and superstitious. Luckily, in recent years scholars have been

opposite:
Three women getting ready for a ceremony dedicated to Bacchus. The Mysteries of Bacchus gave women many opportunities for religious involvement.

259

making good progress in giving us a fairer and more realistic picture of Roman women.

THE VESTAL VIRGINS

As we have seen, political leadership and religious leadership were closely related. Although we know of a few examples of women in public office in cities in Roman-ruled Greece and Asia Minor, there were no government positions open to women in Rome itself. As a result, the roles they could play in the state religion were quite limited. For example, women were rarely, if ever, allowed to preside over blood sacrifices. However, Rome had one priesthood of women that was considered all-important to the well-being of the city and empire. The women of this priesthood were known as Vestal Virgins.

There were six Vestal Virgins. Chosen for their office between the ages of six and ten, they were from upper-class families and had to be physically perfect and to have both parents still living. They went to live at the House of Vesta in the Forum, where they would spend a total of thirty years: ten being trained, ten actively performing religious duties, and ten teaching the younger Vestals. During this time, they could not have any relationships with men. If they did, they were put on trial by the pontiffs and executed if found guilty. After their thirty years of service, they were free to return to their family homes and get married. Most, however, chose to remain in the House of Vesta. As Dionysius of Helicarnassus observed, "The Vestal Virgins receive many fine honors from the city and do not therefore yearn for children or marriage."

Vestals did enjoy privileges that most other Roman women did not. A Vestal was freed from her father's authority and could make a will and give legal testimony without a guardian's oversight. Like a male officeholder, a Vestal had an attendant called a lictor walk before her when she went out. If she happened to come upon a criminal being led to execution, he was immediately pardoned because of the power of her sacred presence. Prime seats were even reserved for the Vestals in the theater. The state paid them a salary that covered all their living expenses and then some. The Vestal Virgins, in fact, made up Rome's only full-time, paid priesthood.

The goddess Vesta (seated) with four Vestal Virgins

These honors came to the Vestals because their duties were believed to guarantee the health and safety of the state. They participated in important processions and ceremonies. They made the *mola salsa* that was used in major sacrifices. They guarded the city's most ancient holy objects, said to have been brought from Troy by Aeneas himself. Most importantly, the Vestals tended the eternal flame of the sacred fire in the temple of Vesta. This was the hearth fire of all Romans, and as long as it continued to burn, Rome would stay strong.

PRIESTESSES AND WORSHIPPERS

Just as many emperors were deified after death, so were some empresses, and honor might be paid to an empress's *iuno* just as to an emperor's *genius*. Some women in the imperial family acted as priestesses in the worship of the deified emperors and empresses. It

Three priestesses taking part in a procession

appears that quite a few women in the eastern part of the empire, and even in some Italian towns, were priestesses responsible for honoring the imperial *genius* and *iuno*. For example, an inscription commemorates an Italian woman named Cassia Cornelia, "priestess of Augusta [a title of the empress] and our fatherland." Such women were leading citizens of their communities. They were also extremely wealthy—part of their priestly role involved paying for sacrifices, religious festivals, and public entertainments. Often these women's husbands also served in the imperial worship, but it seems that many or most of the priestesses held their titles and offices in their own right.

In Greece and Asia Minor, women could be priestesses of Greek gods or goddesses, especially of Artemis, goddess of women, mothers, the moon, and the wilderness. These same women often served in the imperial worship as well. The city of Perge in Asia Minor erected a statue to Plancia Magna, with an inscription on its base reading,

PRIESTESS OF ARTEMIS
AND BOTH FIRST AND SOLE PUBLIC PRIESTESS
OF THE MOTHER OF THE GODS
FOR THE DURATION OF HER LIFE
PIOUS AND PATRIOTIC

A second-century marble bust of a woman named Melitene, who was a priestess of the goddess Cybele

Plancia Magna gave her city a magnificent entrance gate that was decorated with statues and inscriptions honoring two deified emperors, a deified empress, and the reigning emperor and empress.

Women involved in the Mysteries of Demeter, Bacchus, Cybele, and Isis sometimes had the opportunity to become priestesses. Even those who did not take these leadership roles could still dedicate themselves to their beloved deity through initiation. Isis was especially attractive to women, who were given more respect and authority in the worship of this goddess than in any other sphere of Roman life. Isis was called the goddess of women, and at least one hymn to her proclaimed that she made women equal to men. She also embraced all social classes, including slaves and ex-slaves.

Isis was worshipped not only in private initiations but also in public ceremonies. For example, people gathered at her temple in Rome to sing

This woman, taking part in the Mysteries of Bacchus, may be dancing with a veil.

hymns every day as the doors were being opened in the morning and closed in the afternoon. And here is Apuleius's description of some of the women participating in a procession during a festival of Isis:

Women glowing in their white vestments moved with symbolic gestures of delight. Blossomy with the chaplets [wreaths] of the Spring, they scattered flowerets out of the aprons of their dresses. . . . Others, who bore polished mirrors on their backs, walked before [the statue of] the Goddess and reflected all the people coming-after as if they were advancing towards the Image. Others, again, carrying combs of ivory, went through the various caressive motions of combing and dressing the queenly tresses of their Lady; or they sprinkled the street with drops of unguent [perfumed oil]. . . . Then there came walking a great band of men and women of all classes and ages, who had been initiated into the Mysteries of the Goddess and who were all clad in linen garments of the purest white.

Women's religious activities were not limited to priesthoods or to the Mysteries. Although fathers played the main role in family worship, mothers did take part by tending the hearth, helping to take care of

❧ SULPICIA AT JUNO'S TEMPLE ❧

Sulpicia, a first-century B.C.E. poet, is the only Roman woman whose literary works have come down to us today. The following poem may have been written by one of the men who belonged to the same literary circle as Sulpicia, or it may be one that she wrote about herself. In either case, it gives us a marvelous picture of a young Roman woman celebrating her birthday with a visit to Juno's temple.

Juno of birthdays, accept the heaps of holy frankincense
That the learned girl gives to you with tender hand.
Today all is for you; for you, she has most joyously arrayed herself
That, worthy to be seen, she may stand before your altars.
Certainly, Goddess, you are the reason she is all dressed up—
There is, however, one other she secretly would like to please.
But you, Holy One, be favorable, so that no one may tear lovers apart,
And prepare the same bonds for the young man as for her.
You'll do well to unite them this way: there's no more deserving girl
For him to serve, no worthier man for her. . . .
Grant your approval and come, in your radiant purple robe:
Three times offering will be made to you with cake, Pure Goddess, three times
With unmixed wine. And the eager mother advises her daughter what to pray for;
The girl asks something else now, silently in her mind. . . .
And may you also be gracious to the youth, so that when next year comes,
This same longstanding love may still live in their prayers.

the *lararium,* and similar activities. Women could attend sacrifices and other public ceremonies of the state religion, even if their only role (as for most of the other people present) was to watch and keep silent. There were many goddesses whom women particularly favored and who were especially concerned with women's lives. On special occasions and in times of need, women commonly prayed and made offerings at the temples of these much-loved goddesses.

·VI·

THROUGH LIFE'S STAGES

THEY BELIEVED THAT THE GODS TOOK PART
IN ALL THEIR CONCERNS, AT ALL TIMES.
—PLINY THE ELDER, *NATURAL HISTORY*

The Romans felt that unseen powers were all around them. Some, like the great gods, were interested in humans and their cares. Others were impersonal spirits or natural forces. Since these could still affect humans, for good or ill, it was important to behave properly toward them. Things like illness, bad luck, and envy were also powerful forces, and these had to be guarded against. The awareness that gods and spirits of various kinds were always present and active determined many of the customs that accompanied the Romans through the stages of their lives.*

*The customs and traditions we know about are mainly those of the upper class. Very few people outside of this class had the opportunity to record their beliefs, thoughts, feelings, and experiences. In fact, most people in the Roman Empire did not know how to read or write.

This scene from a myth about the birth of Jupiter shows how a newborn Roman baby, wrapped in swaddling clothes, was presented to the father for the first time.

BIRTH AND CHILDHOOD

In the ancient world, childbirth could be a dangerous and frightening experience. Medical knowledge was limited, so many mothers and babies died during or soon after birth. Infants born healthy might not stay that way for long: nearly half of Roman children did not reach their tenth birthday. Given this situation, parents often sought divine help to protect their children.

Women prayed to Diana, Juno Lucina, or a water goddess named Egeria to give them safe pregnancies, easy labors, and healthy babies. For several nights after the birth, three men of the household carried out a protective ceremony, striking the threshold with an axe, then with a pestle, then sweeping the threshold with a broom. The *numina* of these tools of civilization would defend the newborn from Silvanus and other wild spirits. For further divine protection, the family set up a bed for Juno and a table for Hercules in the atrium, as well as a table where the mother's friends could leave offerings for the gods.

Eight days after birth for a girl, and nine for a boy, the baby was purified and named. At this time, many Romans believed, goddesses of fate would decide the child's destiny. Family members were on the lookout for bolts of lightning or other signs from the gods that might give them a hint of what the baby's future held.

Every stage of a child's development was watched over or empowered by a particular deity or *numen*. There were, for exam-

✒ BIRTHDAY PORRIDGE ✒

Birthdays were important family occasions for Romans of all ages. The traditional food for these celebrations was pottage, or porridge. Pliny the Elder explained that the early Romans "lived for a long time not on bread but on pottage. . . . Consequently the oldest sacred rites and birthdays are celebrated with sacrificial pottage."

We might not know how to make sacrificial pottage today, but several other Roman pottage recipes have come down to us. Most combine unground, boiled spelt (a red-grained wheat) with olive oil, spices, and peas or lentils. Some versions add ground meat and a little wine to the mix. Here is an adaptation of a Roman cookbook's recipe for a slightly different, but easy-to-make kind of pottage:

Pultes Tractogalatae (Bread and Milk Porridge)
Put a pint of milk and a little water into a saucepan and warm over low heat. Crumble three pieces of dry bread and add them to the milk. Gently stir from time to time. When the mixture is heated through, add honey to make the porridge as sweet as you want it. *Gusta!* (Taste and enjoy!)

ple, Edusa and Potina to teach it to eat and drink; Ossipago and Carna to strengthen its bones and muscles; Fabulinus and Locutius to help it speak, first in single words and then in sentences; Numeria to help it learn to count; and Camena to teach it to sing.

Along with appealing to the appropriate deities or *numina*, parents had their children wear a *bulla*, the round pendant meant to protect them from the destructive force of envy and other evils. Children also dressed in purple-bordered togas, like those worn by priests, to mark them as holy. And of course, parents were careful to teach their children proper *pietas* so that they would be able to do their part to maintain the *pax deorum* when they grew up.

BECOMING AN ADULT

At around sixteen, a boy had his coming-of-age ceremony. Roman families often chose to celebrate this occasion on March 17, the festival of Liber, a god concerned with the growth of both humans and crops. The boy put aside his childhood clothes and for the first time donned the white toga of manhood. He took off his *bulla* and left it in the *lararium* as an offering to the family's guardian spirits. Then he, his parents, and their friends went to the forum, where he was formally enrolled as a citizen. At the Capitol they made sacrifices to Jupiter and the goddess Iuventas (Youth). The celebration was completed with a feast held at the entrance to the family home—presumably so that everyone passing by would know the boy had become a man. The young man and his family celebrated again when he had his first shave, around the age of twenty-one. The shaved-off beard was offered to the Lares.

There was no coming-of-age ceremony for girls, who might marry as young as twelve. A wedding day had to be chosen carefully, because many days (including the entire month of May) were unlucky for beginning a marriage. The night before a girl's wedding, she gave her *bulla* to the Lares while her father made an offering of incense. At or before dawn the next day, her mother helped her dress in her bridal clothes, which included a straight white tunic and a yellow-orange veil. Her hair was arranged in a style said to symbolize modesty (it was the same hairstyle worn by the Vestals), and she also wore a wreath made of herbs and flowers that were considered lucky.

The wedding ceremony took place at the bride's home. It began with an animal sacrifice and could not continue until a *haruspex*

A nineteenth-century artist painted this scene of a Roman bride, her new husband beside her, making an offering.

examined the internal organs and announced that the gods approved of the marriage. Then a married woman joined together the right hands of the bride and groom, and they stated their consent to be married. A procession accompanied by singers, flute players, and torchbearers led the bride to the groom's house. He carried her over the threshold so that she would not stumble, which would foretell bad luck for the marriage. Next the new wife ceremoniously offered her husband fire and water, symbols of the necessities of life and also of the elements that come together to create new life. After this he presented her to his Lares, and then the wedding feast could begin.

DEATH

People had different ideas about the reasons for life's difficulties. For some, it was a matter of fate. For others, what happened to them was simply due to random chance or luck. To the philosopher-emperor Marcus Aurelius, fate and luck operated together with the gods: "The work of the gods is full of Providence [Fate]: the work of Fortune is not divorced from nature or the spinning and winding of the threads ordained by Providence." Another popular opinion was that problems were the gods' way of testing and strengthening humans. To this idea, Seneca the Younger added, "It is not what you endure, but how you endure it that is important."

One way or another, though, death finally came to everyone. The spirit Caeculus took away the dead person's sight, and Viduus separated the soul from the body. Members of the household laid out the corpse, washed it, and perfumed it with cedar oil, honey, and myrrh. The body was then placed on a flower-decked bed in the atrium, where incense was constantly kept burning. Women

Musicians often accompanied funeral processions.

were hired to lament the deceased, often to the accompaniment of flute players. After a week, the funeral procession set out for the family tomb. Escorting the deceased were musicians, torchbearers, and men carrying the masks or busts of the ancestors. The children of the dead person marched along dressed all in black.

At or near the tomb, the body was laid on a funeral pyre and cremated. Then family members sprinkled the ashes with wine and milk, dried them, and put them into a marble urn in the tomb. After circling the tomb three times and calling out a last farewell to the deceased, they returned home. They sacrificed a ram to the Lares, then shared the traditional funeral meal of eggs, beans, lentils, and chicken. For nine more days of mourning, none of the family did any work. At the end of this period, wine and milk were offered to the spirits of the dead, and then the survivors could resume their normal lives.

People had varying ideas about what happened after death. The most common belief was that the spirits of the dead lived on in the underworld, which they could occasionally leave to interact with the living. These spirits were called the Manes (MAH-nays) or *divi parentes,* "divine ancestors." They were honored at major Roman festivals every year.

RELIGION

VII

ROMAN HOLIDAY

THIS IS A SACRED DAY. PLOUGHMAN AND EARTH MUST REST,
THE HEAVY PLOUGHSHARE HANG AT REST ON THE WALL.
UNHARNESS ALL THE YOKES: LET THE OXEN STAND AND FEAST
AT THE FULL MANGER, WEARING CROWNS OF FLOWERS.
EVERYTHING MUST KEEP HOLIDAY.
—TIBULLUS, *ELEGIES*

There were many religious observances throughout the year. Some were full-blown festivals lasting an entire day or more, when no business was conducted and people gathered together for ceremonies and celebrations. Other occasions were half-day holidays. Most festivals occurred on the same date every year, but some were "movable feasts" (like modern Easter) whose exact date each year had to be set by the pontiffs. Unscheduled festivals could be declared, too—for example, to celebrate a military victory. Most official holidays fell on odd-numbered days, which were considered luckiest. State holidays were celebrated publicly with sacrifices and often with *ludi,* or games. These included chariot races, theatrical

opposite: Women, girls, and musicians on their way to the temple of Ceres to celebrate a springtime holiday.

✑ LET THE GAMES BEGIN! ✑

It can be difficult today to understand exactly how chariot races and similar events related to religion. Even for many Romans during the time of the emperors, the games were more important as a source of entertainment than as a religious observance. Nevertheless, honoring the gods with games was one of the traditional ways of reinforcing the *pax deorum*. The religious aspect of the games was made clear by the processions that began the events. Before a day of chariot racing, "floats" with statues of various deities entered the circus, or stadium, and went around the track. Ovid, famous for his long poems about mythology and love, described such a procession, including his personal thoughts during it. (He, or the character speaking in the selection, seems to have his mind on other things.)

Pay attention! It's time for applause. The golden procession has arrived. Victory is riding in front, her wings outstretched. Be with me, Victory, and make me victorious in love. You who trust yourselves to the sea can clap for Neptune. I have no interest in seafaring; I'm a landlubber. And you, there, soldier, clap for Mars, your patron god. I hate warfare. It's peace I like, and it's in peace that you find love. Let Phoebus [Apollo] help the augurs, and Phoebe [Diana] the hunters. Minerva, seek applause from the craftsmen. Farmers, stand up! Here comes Ceres and delicate Bacchus. Boxers should show reverence to Pollux and horsemen to Castor. Now it's my turn to applaud, sweet Venus, for you and your archer cupids. Nod in support of my plans, oh goddess. Make my new girlfriend receptive to my advances and willing to be loved.

productions, and other spectacles. Admission was free, and vast crowds attended.

The Romans also recognized private holidays, which were family occasions, such as birthdays. (The emperor's birthday, however, called for a grand public celebration.) All important family events were generally marked by prayers to the Lares and Penates. In addition, families gave special worship to these spirits on the first of each month (called the Kalends), roughly a week later (the Nones), and in the middle of the month (the Ides). On these days, the mother decorated the hearth with flower garlands, and the father burned incense and made other offerings to the family guardians. Typical offerings, especially on the Kalends, were honeycombs, grapes, and cakes. The poet Tibullus, away from home, fondly recalled these occasions: "If only I could once again celebrate the Penates of my ancestors, and each month pay homage of incense to the ancient Lar!"

MONTH BY MONTH

Many Roman holidays are difficult to understand today, even for scholars. People often wonder what a particular holiday was about, what its meaning was, or what worshippers were seeking through their actions. In a number of cases, by the time of the emperors the answers to these questions had been forgotten by the Romans themselves. For most Romans, it was enough to know that their ancestors had celebrated these same holidays, with the same ceremonies, for generation after generation. One of the best ways to maintain the *pax deorum* was to keep tradition alive.

All the same, at least some of the reasons for a number of the year's festivities seem clear. For example, the names of many of the months can tell us a lot about what deities were especially honored then and what types of ceremonies took place. The agricultural cycle was also extremely important, because even the most city-bred Romans were well aware that they depended on the earth's production of crops.

January was named after Janus, the god of beginnings, gates, and doorways. His festival, January 1, marked the start of the new year. People celebrated by giving one another small gifts and were careful to speak only of good things all day. On January 3, the Arval Brotherhood vowed sacrifices to the Capitoline Triad and other deities for the well-being of the emperor and his family during the coming year; they also carried out the sacrifices that they had vowed the previous January. Around the same time, Compitalia was celebrated so that people could honor the Lares of the crossroads. January 11 brought Carmentalia, dedicated to Carmentis, a goddess who presided over birth. Toward the end of the month came Sementivae, a country festival that prepared seeds for sowing, with prayers and sacrifices to Ceres and Mother Earth.

Ceres, with the wheat that was her special concern, by an eighteenth-century painter

Februa meant "offerings for purification," and this was a theme in February's major festivals. February 15 was Lupercalia. Priests called Luperci (literally, "wolfmen") made a sacrifice at the place where Rome's founder, Romulus, and his brother, Remus, were said to have been nursed by a wolf after being abandoned in the wilderness. Following the sacrifice, the Luperci, clothed in goatskin, ran through the streets of Rome. Crowds turned out to watch them, and they struck everyone they met with goatskin thongs. This was an act of purification, and people also believed that it would help women who were having trouble becoming pregnant.

Roman festivals sometimes overlapped one another, and Lupercalia came in the middle of Parentalia, February 13–21. The dead were said to wander freely during Parentalia. Temples were closed, but people set out offerings of food and flowers for the dead and held feasts at the tombs of their ancestors. Then, on the twenty-second, Caristia was devoted to renewing family ties, patching up quarrels, and honoring the Lares.

Mars was the namesake of March, when his priests performed their leaping dance on two different holidays and military trumpets were purified. April seems to have been Venus's month and was the favorite time for Roman weddings. In the countryside, agricultural activities were really getting under way, so April also saw a number of festivals related to the earth and farming—for example, the seven-day Cerialia, devoted to the grain goddess Ceres. April 21 was Parilia, in rural Italy a festival to honor the divine guardian of shepherds and their flocks. This was also the official date of Rome's founding, so in the city people celebrated Rome's birthday. Both the rural and urban festivities featured bonfires that people leaped over for good luck.

Flora, the goddess of flowers, painted by the great Renaissance artist Titian

Floralia, the feast of the flower goddess Flora, began on April 28 and lasted through May 3. May was named after Maia, a goddess of growing things. She was said by some to be the mother of Mercury, who shared a festival with Jupiter on May 15. Before this, however, came Lemuria, when fathers protected their households from troublesome ghosts. The end of the month brought Ambarvalia. For this festival of purification, people called on Ceres, Bacchus, Jupiter, Mars, and Janus. To drive away harmful forces, farmers led a sheep, a pig, and an ox around the boundary of their fields; in the city, the same three animals were led around the *pomerium*. The animals were then sacrificed, and the rest of the day was spent in feasting and merrymaking.

So the year went, each month with its festivals to honor the gods, the land, and the history of Rome. The year ended with the most joyous holiday of all, Saturnalia. It began on December 17 and continued through the 23rd. On the first day, there was a sacrifice at the temple of Saturn with a public feast afterward. During the festival, people wore bright-colored clothes, went to parties, exchanged gifts and good wishes, and gave their slaves time off. The author Macrobius recorded that, in addition, "households faithful to the rites honour their slaves by serving them dishes first as if they were the masters." Everyone wore a soft felt cap like the one that was traditionally given to freed slaves, perhaps to show that during this time of year, at least, all human beings were equal. The festival was held in honor of the god Saturn, who was said to have been the first ruler of Italy, the one who gave people laws and taught them how to plant crops. As Virgil wrote, "His reign was the period called in legend the Golden Age, / So peacefully serene were the lives of his subjects."

WOMEN'S FESTIVALS

Some Roman holidays were mainly for women, or involved their active participation. This was especially true for matrons—freeborn married women—particularly those in the upper class. The holiday of Matronalia, on March 1, was dedicated to them and was rather

Women visit a temple of Venus in this scene imagined by a nineteenth-century painter.

like Mother's Day. Women received gifts from their husbands and children; during the reign of Vespasian, the emperor himself gave presents to Rome's matrons. The women visited Juno's temple and offered flowers there.

The first of April was the Veneralia, and matrons went to the temple of Venus Verticordia, "Turner of Hearts," who strengthened marriages. Worshippers washed and dressed Venus's statue in the temple and drank a beverage made of milk, honey, and poppy seeds. Also on April 1, lower-class women honored Fortuna Virilis, the goddess of the Luck of Men, with ceremonies held in public bathhouses. The goddess of the Luck of Women—Fortuna Muliebris—doesn't seem to have had a particular holiday. But the empress Livia, Augustus's third wife, was especially devoted to her and renovated her temple just outside of Rome.

RELIGION

The Vestalia arrived on June 9. On this occasion, Roman matrons took offerings to the temple of Vesta and were allowed into the holiest part of it, usually open only to the Vestal Virgins. The Matralia on June 11 was the day of Mater Matuta, Mother of the Dawn. Matrons celebrated it with their sisters and prayed for the well-being of one another's children. On August 13, there was a festival of Diana. Women wearing flower garlands went in a torch-lit procession to Diana's sanctuary in the grove of Nemi to thank her for answered prayers.

December 3 brought the festival of Bona Dea (the Good Goddess), which matrons and the Vestal Virgins celebrated in the home of a leading government official. All males, including children and slaves, had to leave before preparations could even begin. Then the official's wife or mother decorated the house with vines and other greenery. Priestesses of Bona Dea, who were ex-slaves, brought the statue of the goddess from her temple for the occasion and probably also took part in the ceremonies. These were held at night, and the celebration included a feast, music, singing, and dancing. Many people believed that if these festivities were disturbed or interrupted, the well-being of all Romans would be endangered.

·VIII·

CONFLICT AND TOLERANCE

THROUGHOUT THE WHOLE FAR-FLUNG EMPIRE, . . .
WE SEE THAT EACH LOCAL GROUP OF PEOPLE
HAS ITS OWN RELIGIOUS RITUALS AND WORSHIPS LOCAL GODS. . . .
THE ROMANS, HOWEVER, WORSHIP ALL THE GODS IN THE WORLD.
—MINUCIUS FELIX, *OCTAVIUS*

Rome's religion developed over centuries, and was continuously evolving. With their value for tradition, the Romans rarely dropped time-honored religious practices, but they generally had no problem adding on new gods, new holidays, and new ceremonies or prayers. When Rome conquered a territory, often the deities of that place were formally invited to join the Roman gods. And generally, the residents of conquered lands were permitted to continue their own traditional worship. Emperors even instructed provincial governors to preserve the local holy places.

Under Roman influence, however, the native deities of many provinces underwent a transformation, becoming more Roman

This statue from Gaul, made not long after the region was conquered by Rome, probably depicts a mother goddess and her divine child.

themselves. This happened most obviously in Gaul (modern France and Belgium) and Britain. Before conquest, people in these provinces seldom carved stone images of their deities. After conquest, sculptures of British and Gaulish deities became quite common. The gods and goddesses were frequently portrayed wearing Roman clothing and hairstyles. Often they received Roman names as well, added to their original name and based on the Roman deity to whom they seemed most similar. So, for example, the British goddess Sul became Sul Minerva. A great many British and Gaulish gods were identified with Mars, Mercury, Jupiter, and Apollo, resulting in "combination gods" such as Mars Camulos, Mercury Artaios, Jupiter Taranis, and Apollo Belenus.

One thing that Roman authorities could not accept either in the provinces or at home was a threat to order. There was a difference between religion, which followed proper forms, and superstition. To the Romans, superstition was irrational, overly emotional devotion that resulted in worshippers thinking more of themselves and the otherworld than of the community and this world. This posed one kind of threat. Another came from religious groups, such as the Mysteries, that had their own organization independent of the state. Emperors often feared that any group—religious or otherwise—with its own leaders and treasury might oppose government authority or even start a rebellion. A few religious communities, it seems, did in fact agitate to overthrow Roman rule in some provinces. For all these reasons, emperors from time to time tried to suppress (often violently) or regulate various religious groups, including Isis worshippers, the Druid priesthood of Gaul and Britain, and Christians.

RELIGION AND PATRIOTISM

When Jesus of Nazareth said, "Render to Caesar* the things that are Caesar's, and to God the things that are God's," he was expressing a separation of government and religion that was totally new. For the ancient Romans, it was perfectly natural for religion and politics to mix. As we have seen, they firmly believed that proper worship of the gods was necessary for the well-being of the city and the entire empire. Participating in the public ceremonies of the state religion was an act of patriotism. Refusing to take part in these rites could be seen as an act of treason. This attitude was problematic for Jews and Christians, who acknowledged only one god and often felt that participating in Roman ceremonies was a betrayal of their beliefs.

Roman soldiers in a triumphal procession carry a menorah and other objects looted from the Temple in Jerusalem.

The Roman authorities tended to be more tolerant of Jews than of Christians. Even though Jewish beliefs and practices were very different from Roman ones, Judaism was understandable as the traditional religion of a particular people. Nevertheless, there were individuals in the Roman Empire who were terribly prejudiced, even to the point of violence, against Jews. And when the Jewish province of Judaea rebelled against Roman rule in 66–73 C.E., the empire was merciless. Roman troops destroyed the Temple in Jerusalem, the Jews' most sacred place, forever changing the nature of Jewish religious practice.

*Caesar was used as a title for all Roman emperors.

THE EMPEROR AND THE JEWISH COMMUNITY

Jews lived throughout the Roman Empire, but many of their beliefs and customs—especially their belief in one god—set them apart from their neighbors. Jews generally did not try to win converts and simply wished to be allowed to practice their religion in peace. Unfortunately, there were always people who were suspicious of them because of their different customs. Emperors varied in their attitudes toward the Jewish community. The Jewish philosopher Philo, in a letter to the third emperor, Gaius Caligula, reminded him of the first emperor's tolerance:

Augustus knew that a large part of Rome . . . was occupied and inhabited by Jews. . . . They were not forced to violate their ancestral traditions. Augustus knew that they have places for prayer meetings and that they meet together in these places, especially on the holy sabbaths when they come together as a group to learn their ancestral philosophy. He also knew that they take a first-fruit collection to raise money for religious purposes, and that they send this money to Jerusalem with people who will offer sacrifices. However, he did not banish them from Rome or deprive them of their Roman citizenship just because they were careful to maintain their identities as Jews. He did not force them to abandon their places for prayer meetings, or forbid them to gather to receive instruction in the laws, or oppose their first-fruit collections.

Augustus's successor, Tiberius, was less tolerant. He banished Jews, worshippers of Isis, and astrologers from the city of Rome. Although Gaius Caligula did reestablish the worship of Isis, he did not grant Jews the respect and tolerance requested by Philo. The fourth emperor, Claudius, expelled Christians from Rome (for "causing disturbances," according to the historian Suetonius), but seems to have been more generous toward Jewish communities outside the capital. Following is part of a letter he wrote to the people of Alexandria, Egypt, after a wave of violent conflicts between the Greek and Jewish populations in that city:

Once again I conjure [urge] you that on the one hand the Alexandrians show themselves forbearing and kindly towards the Jews, who for many years have dwelt in the same city, and dishonor none of the rites observed by them in the worship of their god, but allow them to observe their customs as in the time of the deified Augustus, which customs I also, after hearing both sides, have sanctioned; and on the other hand I explicitly order the Jews not to agitate for more privileges than they formerly possessed. . . . If . . . you consent to live with mutual forbearance and kindliness, I on my side will exercise a solicitude of very long standing for the city, as one which is bound to us by traditional friendship.

Christianity was a new religion, without the respectability of a long history. Moreover, Christians actively worked to convince people to join them. This sort of thing had been almost unknown in the Greco-Roman world, and many people were highly offended by Christian efforts to make converts. Some Christians were very vocal about their contempt for traditional Roman religion, and some made a public point of refusing to honor the gods and the emperor's *genius*. To make matters worse, there were a few Christians who preached that the empire was evil and had to be destroyed so that the kingdom of God could be established on earth. When Roman authorities encountered such ideas, they decided that Christians were dangerous rebels.

Christians were first persecuted during the reign of the emperor Nero (54–68 C.E.), when he accused them of starting a fire that destroyed more than half of the city of Rome.

The historian Tacitus described what happened next:

People who admitted their belief were arrested, and then later, through their information, a huge crowd was convicted not so much of the crime of setting the fire, as of hating humankind. Mockery was heaped upon them as they were killed. . . . Nero offered his garden for this spectacle and provided circus entertainment where he put on a chariot driver's outfit and mingled with the crowd or stood in a chariot. And so pity arose, even for those who were guilty . . . since they seemed to have been slaughtered not for public good but to satisfy the cruelty of one man.

Fortunately, such persecutions were relatively rare, at least in the first two centuries C.E. Christians made up a very small percentage of the empire's population, and Roman authorities were generally content to leave them alone so long as they didn't cause any trouble.

THE IMMORTAL GODS

Most Romans felt that Jews and Christians were extremely intolerant to insist on the existence and worship of only one god. Traditional Roman religion, along with the Mysteries, remained strong throughout the 300s. By the 320s, however, the emperor Constantine was favoring Christianity over other religions. All but one of the emperors who came after him were Christians. Still, the vast majority of the empire's residents remained true to their ancient beliefs and practices. Emperors resorted to various techniques, including violence and persecution, to make their subjects convert to Christianity. In 391, Emperor Theodosius I

The Roman gods have lived on in artwork through the centuries. This statue of Bacchus is by Michelangelo.

outlawed all worship of the Roman deities and closed their temples. Yet even after this, devotion to the gods lived on, widespread and fairly open, for at least another century. Other changes came, especially following the fall of Rome in 476. Over the centuries, Christianity became more and more firmly entwined with the culture of Europe and, eventually, the Americas. But the names of our months have not changed since Roman times. People have continued to read the stories of Rome's deities in ancient works such as Virgil's *Aeneid* and Ovid's *Metamorphoses*. Images of the goddesses and gods continue to live, too, in countless beautiful paintings and sculptures. Even for people who no longer believe in these deities, there is still much to admire and much that can inspire.

Most inspiring of all, perhaps, is the vision of a world where people of many backgrounds and faiths can look past their differences, see their common humanity, and live together in harmony. This was the vision of Quintus Aurelius Symmachus. In 384 C.E., he pleaded with the emperor Valentinian II not to persecute the ancient Roman religion: "We are asking for amnesty for the gods of our fathers, the gods of our homeland." His eloquent defense of religious tolerance continued, in words that echo through the centuries:

This Roman copy of a Greek statue remains one of the most famous and well-loved images of the goddess Diana.

It is reasonable to assume that whatever each of us worships can be considered one and the same. We look up at the same stars, the same sky is above us all, the same universe encompasses us. What difference does it make which system each of us uses to find the truth? It is not by just one route that man can arrive at so great a mystery.

GLOSSARY

amphitheater an oval stadium, mainly for shows involving combat or wild-animal fights

aqueduct an artificial channel to carry water from its source to a city

arena an amphitheater's central, ground-level area, where the spectacles took place

atrium the front room of a Roman house, used as a living room and a place to receive visitors

augur a Roman priest with the responsibilities of marking out sacred space and of interpreting the will of the gods

auspices signs from the gods, particularly as observed in the behavior of birds within an area defined by the augurs

bailiff a landowner's agent, who managed all or part of his property for him

barbarian a person whose language could not be understood. For the Romans, barbarians were people and nations who did not speak Latin or Greek and did not share in Greco-Roman culture—and because of this, they were often believed to be uncivilized and somewhat inferior.

basilica a large rectangular building used for public meetings, law courts, and government offices. In a private home, a basilica was a rectangular meeting room.

brazier a pan to hold smoldering charcoal, usually supported by a tripod or other stand, used as a heat source

circus a long, oval stadium where chariot races were held; a racetrack

consecrate to make holy; to dedicate to religious purposes

dowry money, goods, and/or property that a bride's family gave her to bring into her marriage

duovir a co-mayor in Pompeii and some other Roman cities

equestrians members of Rome's second-highest class, ranking below senators. In general, they were wealthy businessmen. Equestrians comes from *equites* (EH-quee-tays), which literally means "horsemen" or "knights," because in early Roman times these were the men wealthy enough to afford warhorses and equipment for fighting on horseback.

eulogy a speech given at a funeral to praise the dead person. Upper-class Romans often delivered eulogies in the forum and then had them inscribed on marble.

forum the civic center and main meeting place of a Roman city, with government buildings, offices, shops, and temples surrounding a large open area. In Rome itself there were six forums: the ancient original Forum plus additional forums built by Julius Caesar and by the emperors Augustus, Nerva, Vespasian, and Trajan.

freeholders people who owned and farmed their own land; sometimes called smallholders, since such farms were usually just large enough to support a family

fresco a wall painting made on fresh plaster

gladiator a professional fighter (nearly always a slave) trained for combat in the amphitheater

imperium "supreme command"—the power to command troops, interpret the law, and pass judgment (including the death sentence) on offenders

infantry a body of soldiers who fight on foot

inscription words written on or carved into lasting materials such as metal and stone

javelin a type of spear

Latin the Romans' language, and the official language of the empire. Greek was also widely used, especially in the eastern part of the empire.

legate a man who commanded armed forces on behalf of the emperor

legion a unit of the Roman army, made up of about five thousand men

lyre a stringed instrument a bit like a small harp

matron a freeborn married woman

mattock a digging tool similar to a pickax

mola salsa grain that was roasted, ground, and mixed with salt, used to bless sacrificial animals and as an offering on its own

mosaic a picture or design made from small square stones. In cheaper mosaics, the stones might be painted or dyed; the best mosaics used stones in a wide range of natural colors.

orator a person skilled in making speeches

pantomime a balletlike performance in which dancers, accompanied by music, wordlessly acted out stories from myth or legend. The performers were usually slaves and included women as well as men.

patrician a member of the upper class

patron an upper-class Roman who gave financial support and other assistance to lower-ranking men. Patrons who were interested in literature often supported poets and other writers.

peristyle a courtyard or garden area surrounded by a covered walkway

personification an imaginary being that represents a thing or an idea

plebeians commoners; the social class to which most Romans belonged

pontiff a member of a Roman priesthood concerned mainly with religious law. The Latin word is *pontifex*, and the plural form is *pontifices* (pohn-TI-fi-kays).

procurator an official who ran an estate or a mine on behalf of the emperor

propitiate to seek the goodwill of the gods

province a territory of the Roman Empire

relief a form of sculpture in which the images project out from a flat surface

rotunda a very large, round room, typically with a domed roof

sharecropper a farmer who worked land owned by someone else. Instead of paying rent for his farm, a sharecropper gave the landowner a portion of whatever he raised.

shrine a small place of worship, usually either outdoors or set aside inside a larger building (such as a wall niche holding a statue of a deity)

tablinum the office or study of the head of the household

tenant farmer a farmer who rented his farm from a landowner

tribute the taxes—in particular grain and other products—that a province had to pay to the Roman government; also a statement acknowledging someone's worth or virtue

trident a three-pronged spear

villa a country home or estate

wattle and daub a building technique using a framework of wooden posts with flexible sticks woven between them (the wattle), filled in with a mixture of mud, clay, and straw (the daub)

FOR FURTHER READING

Amery, Heather, and Patricia Vanags. *Rome & Romans*. London: Usborne, 1997.

Biesty, Stephen. *Rome in Spectacular Cross-Section*. New York: Scholastic Nonfiction, 2003.

Corbishley, Mike. *What Do We Know about the Romans?* New York: Peter Bedrick Books, 1991.

Dargie, Richard. *A Roman Villa*. Austin and New York: Raintree Steck-Vaughn, 2000.

Denti, Mario. *Journey to the Past: Imperial Rome*. Austin and New York: Raintree Steck-Vaughn, 2001.

Ganeri, Anita. *How Would You Survive as an Ancient Roman?* New York: Franklin Watts, 1995.

Hart, Avery, and Sandra Gallagher. *Ancient Rome! Exploring the Culture, People and Ideas of This Powerful Empire*. Charlotte, VT: Williamson Publishing, 2002.

Hinds, Kathryn. *The Ancient Romans*. New York: Benchmark Books, 1997.

Hodge, Susie. *Ancient Roman Art*. Chicago: Heinemann Library, 1998.

Jovinelly, Joann, and Jason Netelkos. *The Crafts and Culture of the Romans*. New York: Rosen Publishing Group, 2002.

Lassieur, Allison. *The Ancient Romans*. New York: Scholastic, 2005.

Macaulay, David. *City: A Story of Roman Planning and Construction*. Boston: Houghton Mifflin, 1974.

Macdonald, Fiona. *The Roman Colosseum*. New York: Peter Bedrick Books, 1996.

———. *Women in Ancient Rome*. New York: Peter Bedrick Books, 2000.

Mann, Elizabeth. *The Roman Colosseum*. New York: Mikaya Press, 1998.

Markel, Rita J. *The Fall of the Roman Empire*. Minneapolis, MN: Twenty-First Century Books, 2008.

Mellor, Ronald, and Marnie McGee. *The Ancient Roman World*. New York: Oxford University Press, 2004.

Morley, Jacqueline. *A Roman Villa: Inside Story*. New York: Peter Bedrick Books, 1992.

Nardo, Don. *Life in Ancient Rome*. San Diego, CA: Lucent Books, 1997.

———. *Life of a Roman Soldier*. San Diego, CA: Lucent Books, 2001.

———. *The Roman Empire*. San Diego, CA: Lucent Books, 1994.

Seely, John, and Elizabeth Seely. *Pompeii and Herculaneum*. Chicago: Heinemann Library, 2000.

Tanaka, Shelley. *The Buried City of Pompeii: What It Was Like When Vesuvius Exploded*. Toronto: Madison Press Books, 1997.

Whittock, Martyn. *The Colosseum and the Roman Forum*. Chicago: Heinemann Library, 2003.

ONLINE INFORMATION

Carr, Dr. Karen. *History for Kids: Ancient Rome.*
> http://www.historyforkids.org/learn/romans/index.htm

Curran, Leo C. *Maecenas: Images of Ancient Greece and Rome.*
> http://wings.buffalo.edu/AandL/Maecenas/general_contents.html

Devillier Donegan Enterprises. *The Roman Empire in the First Century.*
> http://www.pbs.org/empires/romans

Educational Broadcasting Corporation. *Secrets of the Dead: The Great Fire of Rome.*
> http://www.pbs.org/wnet/secrets/previous_seasons/case_rome/index.html

Educational Broadcasting Corporation. *Warrior Challenge: Romans.*
> http://www.pbs.org/wnet/warriorchallenge/romans

Frischer, Bernard. *Horace's Villa Project.*
> http://www.humnet.ucla.edu/horaces-villa

Goldberg, Dr. Neil. *Rome Project.*
> http://intranet.dalton.org/groups/rome/index.html

Illustrated History of the Roman Empire.
> http://www.roman-empire.net

Michael C. Carlos Museum of Emory University. *Odyssey Online: Rome.*
> http://carlos.emory.edu/ODYSSEY/ROME/homepg.html

Mountain City Elementary School, Mountain City, TN. *Ancient Rome.*
> http://www.mce.k12tn.net/ancient_rome/rome.htm

NOVA Online. *Secrets of Lost Empires: Roman Bath.*
> http://www.pbs.org/wgbh/nova/lostempires/roman

Pollard, Dr. Nigel. *Roman Religion Gallery.*
> http://www.bbc.co.uk/history/ancient/romans/roman_religion_gallery.shtml

Roman Open-Air Museum in Hechingen-Stein.
> http://www.villa-rustica.de/intro/indexe.html

Thayer, William P. *Lacus Curtius: Into the Roman World.*
> http://chnm.gmu.edu/worldhistorysources/r/208/whm.html

SELECTED BIBLIOGRAPHY

Adkins, Lesley, and Roy A. Adkins. *Dictionary of Roman Religion*. New York: Facts on File, 1996.

———. *Handbook to Life in Ancient Rome*. New York and Oxford: Oxford University Press, 1994.

Apuleius. *The Golden Ass*. Translated by Jack Lindsay. Bloomington: Indiana University Press, 1962.

Beard, Mary, et al. *Religions of Rome*. Volume I: *A History*. Cambridge: Cambridge University Press, 1998.

Boardman, John, et al., eds. *The Oxford Illustrated History of the Roman World*. Oxford and New York: Oxford University Press, 1988.

Carcopino, Jerome. *Daily Life in Ancient Rome*. Edited by Henry T. Rowell. Translated by E. O. Lorimer. New Haven, CT: Yale University Press, 1968.

Cornell, Tim, and John Matthews. *The Roman World*. Alexandria, VA: Stonehenge Press, 1991.

Davenport, Basil, ed. *The Portable Roman Reader*. New York: Penguin, 1979.

Editors of Time-Life Books. *Pompeii: The Vanished City*. Alexandria, VA: Time-Life Books, 1992.

———. *Rome: Echoes of Imperial Glory*. Alexandria, VA: Time-Life Books, 1994.

———. *What Life Was Like When Rome Ruled the World: The Roman Empire 100 BC-AD 200*. Alexandria, VA: Time-Life Books, 1997.

Edwards, John. *Roman Cookery: Elegant & Easy Recipes from History's First Gourmet*. Rev. ed. Point Roberts, WA: Hartley & Marks, 1986.

Fantham, Elaine, et al. *Women in the Classical World: Image and Text*. New York and Oxford: Oxford University Press, 1994.

Grabsky, Phil. *I, Caesar: Ruling the Roman Empire*. London: BBC Books, 1997.

Grant, Michael. *The World of Rome*. New York: Praeger Publications, 1969.

Hallett, Judith P. "Women in the Ancient Roman World." In *Women's Roles in Ancient Civilizations: A Reference Guide*, edited by Bella Vivante, 257–289. Westport, CT: Greenwood Press, 1999.

Highet, Gilbert. *Poets in a Landscape*. New York: Alfred A. Knopf, 1957.

James, Peter, and Nick Thorpe. *Ancient Inventions*. New York: Ballantine Books, 1994.

Kamm, Antony. *The Romans: An Introduction*. New York and London: Routledge, 1995.

Kraemer, Ross Shepard. *Her Share of the Blessings: Women's Religions among Pagans, Jews, and Christians in the Greco-Roman World*. New York: Oxford University Press, 1992.

Lewis, C. Day, trans. *The Aeneid of Virgil*. Garden City, NY: Doubleday, 1953.

Lewis, Naphtali, and Meyer Reinhold, eds. *Roman Civilization. Sourcebook II: The Empire*. New York: Harper & Row, 1966.

MacMullen, Ramsay, and Eugene N. Lane. *Paganism and Christianity 100-425 C.E.: A Sourcebook*. Minneapolis, MN: Fortress Press, 1992.

Mellor, Ronald, ed. *The Historians of Ancient Rome: An Anthology of the Major Writings*. New York and London: Routledge, 1998.

Meyer, Marvin W., ed. *The Ancient Mysteries: A Sourcebook*. San Francisco: Harper & Row, 1987.

Santosuosso, Antonio. *Storming the Heavens: Soldiers, Emperors, and Civilians in the Roman Empire*. Boulder, CO: Westview Press, 2001.

Scarre, Chris. *Chronicle of the Roman Emperors: The Reign-by-Reign Record of the Rulers of Imperial Rome*. London: Thames & Hudson, 1995.

Shelton, Jo-Ann. *As the Romans Did: A Source Book in Roman Social History*. 2nd ed. New York and Oxford: Oxford University Press, 1998.

Tacitus. *Dialogus, Agricola, Germania*. Latin text, with facing-page translation by Sir William Peterson. Cambridge, MA: Harvard University Press, 1914.

Turcan, Robert. *The Gods of Ancient Rome: Religion in Everyday Life from Archaic to Imperial Times*. Translated by Antonia Nevill. New York: Routledge, 2000.

Vitruvius. *The Ten Books on Architecture*. Translated by Morris Hicky Morgan. New York: Dover Publications, 1960.

Wells, Colin. *The Roman Empire*. 2nd ed. Cambridge, MA: Harvard University Press, 1992.

White, K. D. *Country Life in Classical Times*. Ithaca, NY: Cornell University Press, 1977.

Zanker, Paul. *Pompeii: Public and Private Life*. Translated by Deborah Lucas Schneider. Cambridge, MA: Harvard University Press, 1998.

SOURCES FOR QUOTATIONS

The Patricians

Chapter I

p. 9 "It became essential": Mellor, *The Historians of Ancient Rome*, p. 478.

p. 12 "Nothing . . . was done": Shelton, *As the Romans Did*, p. 229.

p. 12 "the Romans and their allies": ibid., p. 235.

p. 13 "to make levies": ibid., p. 228.

p. 15 "futility of long speeches": Boardman, *The Oxford Illustrated History of the Roman World*, p. 132.

p. 16 "Even if he did": Scarre, *Chronicle of the Roman Emperors*, p. 95.

Chapter II

p. 18 "But when it comes": Scarre, *Chronicle of the Roman Emperors*, p. 97.

p. 22 "in almost every city": ibid., p. 102.

p. 24 "Because of his shrewd": Shelton, *As the Romans Did*, p. 334.

p. 25 "the enricher": Editors of Time-Life Books, *Rome*, p. 81.

Chapter III

p. 28 "His friends he enriched": Mellor, *The Historians of Ancient Rome*, p. 503.

p. 30 "one of his few": ibid., p. 477.

p. 31 "a poem and a mistake": translation of *"carmen et error,"* Boardman, *The Oxford Illustrated History of the Roman World*, p. 203.

p. 32 "Don't neglect": Shelton, *As the Romans Did*, pp. 51–52.

p. 35 "my partner in toil": Tacitus, *Annals*, quoted in Wells, *The Roman Empire*, p. 105.

p. 35 "He won the heart": Mellor, *The Historians of Ancient Rome*, p. 445.

p. 37 "willingly permitted" and "honoured by": Wells, *The Roman Empire*, p. 115.

Chapter IV

p. 38 "There can be great": Boardman, *The Oxford Illustrated History of the Roman World*, p. 132.

p. 39 "wrote, dictated, listened": Mellor, *The Historians of Ancient Rome*, p. 506.

p. 39 "often bathed": *Augustan Histories*, quoted in Mellor, *The Historians of Ancient Rome*, p. 504.

p. 39 "a stall of marble": Suetonius, *The Life of Gaius Caligula*, quoted in Mellor, *The Historians of Ancient Rome*, p. 389.

p. 41 "daily routine": Kamm, *The Romans*, pp. 68–69.

p. 44 "Let the vigorous": author's translation of Odes, Book 3, Ode 2; original Latin text at http://www.thelatinlibrary.com/horace/carm3.shtml

p. 45 "Though more desirous": Mellor, *The Historians of Ancient Rome*, pp. 499–500.

Chapter V

p. 46 "The emperor repeatedly": Mellor, *The Historians of Ancient Rome*, p. 424.

p. 49 "the one woman": Wells, *The Roman Empire*, p. 19.

p. 51 "best of mothers": Scarre, *Chronicle of the Roman Emperors*, p. 51.

p. 51 "Many years before": Mellor, *The Historians of Ancient Rome*, p. 470.

p. 52 "By heaven": Scarre, *Chronicle of the Roman Emperors*, p. 110.

p. 53 "Rare indeed": Shelton, *As the Romans Did*, p. 292.

p. 53 "My wife is very": ibid., p. 45.

p. 54 "your modesty": ibid., p. 292.

p. 54 "How could the desire": ibid., p. 294.

p. 55 "Ummidia Quadratilla": ibid., pp. 300–301.

Chapter VI

p. 56 "He passed his boyhood": Mellor, *The Historians of Ancient Rome*, p. 395.

p. 58 "Above all, make sure": Shelton, *As the Romans Did*, p. 32.

p. 59 Roman checkers adapted from Wladyslaw Jan Kowalski, *Roman Board Games*, at http://www.aerobiologicalengineering.com /wxk116/Roman/BoardGames

p. 63 "has recently read": Fantham, *Women in the Classical World*, p. 349.

Chapter VII

p. 64 "I admire him": Scarre, *Chronicle of the Roman Emperors*, p. 118.

p. 66 "at some dinner": Grabsky, *I , Caesar*, p. 74.

p. 67 Recipe adapted from Edwards, *Roman Cookery*, p. 76.

p. 69 "The first rule is": Scarre, *Chronicle of the Roman Emperors*, p. 118.

p. 70 "a time when": Kamm, *The Romans*, 83.

p. 71 "the senate-house besieged": Mellor, *The Historians of Ancient Rome*, p. 415.

The City
Chapter I

p. 75 "Even now": author's translation of *Metamorphoses*, Book 15, lines 444–445; original Latin text at http://www.thelatinlibrary.com/ovid/ovid.met15.shtml

p. 76 "Goddess of continents": Carcopino, *Daily Life in Ancient Rome*, p. 21.

p. 78 "Will anybody": Editors of Time-Life Books, *Rome*, p. 154.

p. 79 "the charms" and "Agricola gave": Mellor, *The Historians of Ancient Rome*, p. 404.

p. 81 "I used to": Boardman, *The Oxford Illustrated History of the Roman World*, p. 208.

Chapter II

p. 84 "The Roman people": Vitruvius, *The Ten Books on Architecture*, p. 57.

p. 87 "an admirably large": Grabsky, *I, Caesar*, p. 25.

p. 90 "We inhabit": Carcopino, *Daily Life in Ancient Rome*, p. 32.

p. 92 "because I saw": Vitruvius, *The Ten Books on Architecture*, p. 4.

p. 93 "to suit" and "Men of everyday": ibid., p. 182.

p. 95 "that perfection": ibid., p. 14.

Chapter III

p. 97 "Hello Profit": Shelton, *As the Romans Did*, p. 135.

p. 100 "You cannot control": ibid., p. 176.

p. 100 "I was happy": ibid., pp. 182–183.

p. 102 "The muleteers": Wells, *The Roman Empire*, p. 41.

p. 104 "Grammarian, orator": Boardman, *The Oxford Illustrated History of the Roman World*, p. 341.

p. 104 "Fortune, do you": Shelton, *As the Romans Did*, p. 195.

p. 104 "I hope that": ibid., p. 194.

Chapter IV

p. 107 "If you ask": Shelton, *As the Romans Did*, p. 148.

p. 109 "Once upon": ibid., p. 13.

p. 109 "This morning": Carcopino, *Daily Life in Ancient Rome*, p. 172.

p. 109 "How many": Shelton, *As the Romans Did*, pp. 14–15.

p. 111 "to wear the toga": Mellor, *The Historians of Ancient Rome*, p. 507.

p. 112 "Your teeth": Boardman, *The Oxford Illustrated History of the Roman World*, p. 165.

p. 113 "Then they march": Shelton, *As the Romans Did*, p. 254.

p. 115 "It is chiefly": Mellor, *The Historians of Ancient Rome*, p. 446.

Chapter V

p. 117 "Guardians are appointed": Shelton, *As the Romans Did*, p. 34.

p. 118 "Don't marry": ibid., p. 299.

p. 119 "My dearest mother": Fantham, *Women in the Classical World*, p. 318.

p. 122 "My hateful birthday": ibid., p. 324.

p. 123 "She says that after": ibid., p. 368.

Chapter VI

p. 125 "Praise lifts": Shelton, *As the Romans Did*, p. 31.

p. 126 "If I receive": ibid., p. 28.

p. 128 "Let his lessons": ibid., p. 102.

p. 129 "Viccentia, sweetest": Fantham, *Women in the Classical World*, p. 377.

p. 130 "My father": Shelton, *As the Romans Did*, p. 18.

Chapter VII

p. 133 "Hunting, bathing": Editors of Time-Life Books, *Rome*, p. 117.

p. 136 "I scarcely ever": Shelton, *As the Romans Did*, p. 319.

p. 136 "Their hands": Carcopino, *Daily Life in Ancient Rome*, p. 227.

p. 138 "Here I lie": Shelton, *As the Romans Did*, p. 346.

p. 139 "There was a battle": Scarre, *Chronicle of the Roman Emperors*, p. 73.

p. 140 "There is nothing": Shelton, *As the Romans Did*, p. 355.

Chapter VIII

p. 141 "If there could": Wells, *The Roman Empire*, p. 196.

p. 142 "Water ought": Vitruvius, *The Ten Books on Architecture*, p. 247.

p. 143 "Most sick men": Highet, *Poets in a Landscape*, pp. 221–222.

p. 144 "The blaze": Mellor, *The Historians of Ancient Rome*, pp. 471–472.

p. 146 "On 24 August": Wells, *The Roman Empire*, p. 188.

p. 146 "And now cinders": Editors of Time-Life Books, *Pompeii*, p. 20.

p. 147 "the courtyard": Wells, *The Roman Empire*, p. 188.

p. 147 "The coaches": Editors of Time-Life Books, *Pompeii*, p. 23.

p. 149 "there may be fed": Shelton, *As the Romans Did*, p. 36.

The Countryside
Chapter I

p. 153 "Then let me love": Highet, *Poets in a Landscape*, p. 57.

p. 154 "Through this, Rome became": ibid., p. 59.

p. 154 "Those were the sons": ibid., p. 129.

p. 155 "Happy—even too happy": ibid., p. 57.

p. 156 "From the day": White, *Country Life in Classical Times*, p. 93.

p. 158 "Do you ask": ibid., p. 49.

p. 160 "Up until this day": Shelton, *As the Romans Did*, pp. 286–287.

Chapter II

p. 163 "Hail, earthly paradise": Highet, *Poets in a Landscape*, p. 62.

p. 164 "Often the farmer": White, *Country Life in Classical Times*, p. 10.

p. 165 "It is well known": Tacitus, *Dialogus, Agricola, Germania*,
pp. 287, 301.

p. 166 "Anyone living": Wells, *The Roman Empire*, pp. 227–228.

p. 167 "I always leave": Highet, *Poets in a Landscape*, p. 136.

Chapter III

p. 171 "If we must live": Highet, *Poets in a Landscape*, p. 153.

p. 171 "With [animal] skins": Lewis, *Roman Civilization*, p. 107.

p. 172 "On the other hand": Vitruvius, *The Ten Books on Architecture*,
pp. 39–40.

p. 174 "So, when the gods": White, *Country Life in Classical Times*,
pp. 47–48.

p. 176 "In a poor cottage": Highet, *Poets in a Landscape*, p. 153.

p. 177 "a terrace": Shelton, *As the Romans Did*, p. 77.

p. 177 "Next comes the broad": ibid., p. 77.

p. 178 "The size of a villa": ibid., pp. 72–74.

Chapter IV

p. 181 "The farmer cleaves": Highet, *Poets in a Landscape*, p. 58.

p. 181 "digging and heaving rocks": ibid., p. 137.

p. 181 "We worked hard": White, *Country Life in Classical Times*, p. 73.

p. 182 "I myself never": Shelton, *As the Romans Did*, p. 146.

p. 183 "Their skin was striped": Apuleius, *The Golden Ass*, p. 192.

p. 184 "Without delay the year's": Highet, *Poets in a Landscape*, p. 58.

p. 186 "Olives that can": White, *Country Life in Classical Times*, p. 71.

p. 187 "The type of man": ibid., p. 75.

p. 187 "The slaves engaged": Shelton, *As the Romans Did*, p. 172.

Chapter V

p. 189 "Happy is the man": Shelton, *As the Romans Did*, p. 161.

p. 190 "I am reminded": White, *Country Life in Classical Times*, p. 20.

p. 190 "one way of increasing": ibid., p. 19.

p. 191 "I am totally involved": Boardman, *The Oxford Illustrated History of the Roman World*, p. 353.

p. 192 "Let another man": Shelton, *As the Romans Did*, p. 161.

p. 193 "Simulus, the peasant farmer": ibid., pp. 157–158.

p. 194 "to let out": White, *Country Life in Classical Times*, p. 92.

p. 195 "Winter's the tenant's": ibid., p. 61.

Chapter VI

p. 197 "Delia will guard": Highet, *Poets in a Landscape*, p. 163.

p. 199 "Here I lie": Shelton, *As the Romans Did*, p. 290.

p. 199 "It is incredible": ibid., p. 46.

p. 200 "The handiwork": Highet, *Poets in a Landscape*, p. 168.

pp. 200, 201 "can follow" and "are as good": White, *Country Life in Classical Times*, pp. 75–76.

p. 201 "At one moment": Shelton, *As the Romans Did*, p. 305.

p. 202 "Moreover, they believe": Tacitus, *Dialogus, Agricola, Germania*, pp. 274, 276; author's translation of Latin text.

p. 202 "You have learned": Lewis, *Roman Civilization*, p. 415.

Chapter VII

p. 205 "Fathers order": Shelton, *As the Romans Did*, p. 22.

p. 206 "pregnant women": White, *Country Life in Classical Times*, p. 76.

p. 207 "Ligdus . . . was a poor man": Shelton, *As the Romans Did*, pp. 28–29.

p. 208 "When father was": White, *Country Life in Classical Times*, p. 83.

Chapter VIII

p. 211 "Drive diseases": White, *Country Life in Classical Times*, p. 102.

pp. 211, 212 "took from the fields" and "twigs and shoots": Wells, *The Roman Empire*, p. 246.

p. 212 "If the Romans": Grant, *The World of Rome*, p. 51.

p. 212 "Countless tribes": Lewis, *Roman Civilization*, p. 108.

p. 213 "Yes, even on holy": White, *Country Life in Classical Times*, p. 61.

p. 214 "Hither the farmer's": ibid., p. 100.

p. 215 "Put your hands": Shelton, *As the Romans Did*, p. 381.

Religion

Chapter I

p. 219 "Rome is a place": Turcan, *The Gods of Ancient Rome*, p. 148.

p. 219 "If we compare": ibid., p. 12.

p. 221 "*redire ad Larem suum*": ibid., p. 16.

p. 225 "Alas, I suppose": Adkins, *Dictionary of Roman Religion*, p. 106; author's translation of *Vae puto deus fio*, from Suetonius, *Divus Vespasianus*.

p. 226 "a feeling": MacMullen, *Paganism and Christianity*, p. 81.

p. 227 "Most holy and everlasting": Apuleius, *The Golden Ass*, pp. 250–251.

Chapter II

p. 229 "And what reason": MacMullen, *Paganism and Christianity*, p. 82.

p. 231 "It's not the abundance": *Ancient History Sourcebook* at http://www.fordham.edu/halsall/ancient/personalrelig.html

p. 231 "It apparently does no good": Shelton, *As the Romans Did*, pp. 371–372.

p. 232 "Whether you are a god": ibid., p. 363; author's adaptation of a
    prayer recorded by Cato the Elder in *On Agriculture*.

p. 232 "A memorandum to the god": ibid., p. 14.

p. 233 "There is indeed nobody": MacMullen, *Paganism and Christianity*,
    pp. 22–23.

p. 237 "I approached the confines": Apuleius, *The Golden Ass*, p. 249.

Chapter III

p. 239 "We have a city": Beard, *Religions of Rome*, p. 168.

p. 240 "god-haunted feel": Lewis, *The Aeneid of Virgil*, p. 189.

p. 240 "In this grove": author's translation of *Aeneid*, Book 8, lines
    351–354; original Latin text at
    http://www.thelatinlibrary.com/vergil/aen8.shtml

p. 241 "This will enable": Vitruvius, *The Ten Books on Architecture*, p. 116.

p. 242 "On June 21": Lewis, *Roman Civilization*, pp. 553–554.

p. 245 "There is a fair-sized": Highet, *Poets in a Landscape*, pp. 89–90.

p. 247 "If you have ever": MacMullen, *Paganism and Christianity*, p. 79.

Chapter IV

p. 249 "Each hour be minded": MacMullen, *Paganism and Christianity*,
    p. 107.

p. 251 "O, divine nights": Turcan, *The Gods of Ancient Rome*, p. 17.

p. 251 "With these beans": author's translation of *Fasti*, Book 5, line
    438; original Latin text at
    http://www.thelatinlibrary.com/ovid/ovid.fasti5.shtml

p. 252 "Even to the rural": Turcan, *The Gods of Ancient Rome*, p. 38.

p. 252 "I entrust to your care": Shelton, *As the Romans Did*, p. 369.

p. 253 "Among the many things": Beard, *Religions of Rome*, p. 115.

p. 254 "all the priesthoods": Shelton, *As the Romans Did*, p. 384.

p. 254 "to make sure" and "For private citizens": ibid., p. 385.

Chapter V

p. 259 "Women [are] the chief": Kraemer, *Her Share of the Blessings*, p. 3.

p. 260 "The Vestal Virgins": Shelton, *As the Romans Did*, p. 386.

p. 262 "priestess of Augusta": Fantham, *Women in the Classical World*,
    p. 362.

p. 263 "Priestess of Artemis": ibid., p. 363.

p. 264 "Women glowing": Apuleius, *The Golden Ass*, pp. 240–241.

p. 265 "Juno of birthdays": author's translation of Tibullus, *Elegies*, Book 3, section 12, ©2004 by Kathryn Hinds; original Latin text at http://www.thelatinlibrary.com/tibullus3.html

Chapter VI

p. 267 "They believed": author's translation of *Natural History*, Book 28; original Latin text at http://penelope.uchicago. edu/Thayer/L/ Roman/Texts/Pliny_the_Elder/28*.html

p. 269 "lived for a long time": Edwards, *Roman Cookery*, p. 66.

p. 269 Recipe adapted from Edwards, *Roman Cookery*, p. 66.

p. 272 "The work of the gods": MacMullen, *Paganism and Christianity*, p. 107.

p. 272 "It is not what": Shelton, *As the Romans Did*, p. 430.

Chapter VII

p. 275 "This is a sacred day": Highet, *Poets in a Landscape*, p. 166.

p. 276 "Pay attention!": Shelton, *As the Romans Did*, pp. 340–341.

p. 277 "If only I could": Turcan, *The Gods of Ancient Rome*, p. 29.

p. 280 "households faithful": ibid., p. 35.

p. 280 "His reign was": Lewis, *The Aeneid of Virgil*, p. 189.

Chapter VIII

p. 283 "Throughout the whole": Shelton, *As the Romans Did*, p. 417.

p. 285 "Render to Caesar": Holy Bible, Revised Standard Version, Mark 12:17.

p. 286 "Augustus knew": Shelton, *As the Romans Did*, p. 405.

p. 287 "causing disturbances": ibid., p. 408.

p. 287 "Once again I conjure": MacMullen, *Paganism and Christianity*, pp. 155–156.

p. 288 "People who admitted": Shelton, *As the Romans Did*, p. 409.

p. 290 "We are asking": ibid., p. 391.

p. 291 "It is reasonable": ibid.

INDEX

PICTURE CREDITS

Images provided by Rose Corbett Gordon, Art Editor of Mystic CT, from the following sources:

Front Cover: Villa dei Misteri, Pompeii, Italy/The Bridgeman Art Library
Back cover: The Art Archive/Musée du Louvre Paris/Gianni Dagli Orti

The Patricians Page 1: The Art Archive/Musée Archéologique Naples/Alfredo Dagli Orti; pages 4, 13 left, 14, 27, 29: Scala/Art Resource, NY; page 5: Vanni Archive/CORBIS; page 6: The Bridgeman Art Library/Getty Images; pages 7, 8, 19, 33, 37, 57, 60: Erich Lessing/Art Resource, NY; pages 11, 17 right: Louvre, Paris/Giraudon/Bridgeman Art Library; page 13 right: Private Collection/Bridgeman Art Library; page 17 left: SEF/Art Resource, NY; page 21: Vanni/Art Resource, NY; page 22: Bill Ross/Corbis; page 23: Victoria Art Gallery, Bath and North Fast Somerset Council/Bridgeman Art Library; page 24: Archivo Iconografico, S.A./Corbis; page 25: The Art Archive/Dagli Orti; page 26: Forum, Rome/Giraudon/Bridge¬man Art Library; page 31: Musée National du Bardo, Le Bardo/Giraudon/Bridgeman Art Library; page 32, 70: Gilles Mermet/Art Resource, NY; page 34: The Art Archive/Museo Prenestino Palestrina/Dagli Orti; page 40: Kunsthistorisches Museum, Vienna/Bridgeman Art Library; page 42: Museum of London/Topham/The Image Works; page 44: The Art Archive/Musée du Louvre Paris/Dagli Orti; page 47: Villa dei Misteri, Pompeii, Italy/Bridgeman An Library; page 49: Burstein Collection/Corbis; page 50: Museo Archeologico Nazionale, Naples, Italy/Bridgeman Art Library; page 52: The Art Archive/Archae¬ological Museum Vaison la Romaine/Dagli Orti; page 55: Metropolitan Museum of Art, New York/Bridgeman Art Library; page 58:: The Art Archive/Museo della Civilta Romana Rome/Dagli Orti; page 62: The Art Archive/Musée Lapidaire d'Art Paien Arles/Dagli Orti; page 65: The Art Archive/Bibliothèque des Arts Decoratifs Paris/Dagli Orti.

The City Pages 73, 96, 114, 135, 139: Scala/Art Resource, NY; pages 74, 142: Museo della Civilta Romana, Rome/Giraudon/Bridgeman Art Library; page 77: Private Collection/Christopher Wood Gallery, London/Bridgeman Art Library; page 78: Giraudon/Art Resource, NY; page 79: Verulamium Museum, St. Albans, Hertfordshire, UK/Bridgeman Art Library; pages 81, 85: The Granger Collection, New York; pages 82. 89: Roger Wood/Corbis; page 87: Phillips, The International Fine Art Auctioneers, UK/Bridgeman Art Library; pages 88, 92, 120: Mimmo Jodice/Corbis; pages 91, 102, 138: Araldo de Luca/Corbis; page 93: Gustavo Tomsich/Corbis; pages 94, 113: Werner Forman/Art Resource, NY; page 95: Archivo Iconografico, S.A./Corbis; pages 98, 99, 124, 128: Erich Lessing/Art Resource, NY; page 101: Museo della Civilta Romana, Rome/Bridgeman Art Library; page 103: Musée des Antiquités Nationales, St-Germain-en-Laye, France/Lauros/Giraudon/Bridgeman Art Library; page 106: The Art Archive/Museo della Civilta Romana Rome/Dagli Orti; page 111: Louvre, Paris/Lauros/Giraudon/Bridgeman Art Library; page 116: Villa dei Misteri, Pompeii, Italy/Bridgeman Art Library; page 118: The Art Archive/Museo Nazionale Terme Rome/Dagli Orti; page 121: Alinari/Art Resource. NY; page 122: Sandro Vannini/Corbis; page 127: The Art Archive/Museo della Civilta Romana, Rome/Dagli Orti; page 130: The Art Archive/Archaeological Museum Salonica/Dagli Orti; page 132: Christie's Images/Corbis; page 137: Hulton Archive/Getty Images; page 145; SEF/Art Resource, NY; page 146: Roger Ressmeyer/Corbis.

The Countryside Page 151: Brooklyn Museum of Art, New York/Charles Edwin Wilbour Fund/Bridgeman Art Library; page 152: The Art Archive/Byzantine Mosaic Museum Istanbul/Dagli Orti; pages 155, 208: The Art Archive/Museo della Civilta Romana, Rome/Dagli Orti; pages 157, 160, 187, 192, 209: Erich Lessing/Art Resource, NY; pages 162, 180: Gilles Mermet/Art Resource, NY; page 165: Musée National du Bardo, Le Bardo, Tunisia/Lauros/Giraudon/Bridgeman Art Library; pages 167, 210: The Art Archive/Dagli Orti; page 168: Rome/Index/Bridgeman Art Library; page 170: Archivo Iconografico, S.A./Corbis; pages 174, 184, 213: Scala/Art Resource, NY; pages 176, 201: The Granger Collection, New York; page 177: Villa Romana del Casale, Piazza Armerina, Sicily/Bridgeman Art Library; pages 178, 198: The Art Archive/Archaeological Museum Naples/Dagli Orti; page 183: The Art Archive/Archaeological Museum Tipasa Algeria/Dagli Orti; page 185: Musée des Antiquités Nationales, St-Germain-en-Laye, France/Lauros/Giraudon/Bridgeman Art Library; page 188: Pushkin Museum, Moscow/Bridgeman Art Library; page 191: Ashmoleon Museum, Oxford/Bridgeman Art Library; page 196: Gaziantep Archaeological Museum, Gaziantep, Turkey/Bridgeman Art Library; page 199: The Art Archive/Archaeological Museum Naples/Dagli Orti; page 202: The Stapleton Collection/Bridgeman Art Library; page 204: Mimmo Jodice/Corbis; page 206: Alinari

Archives/Corbis; page 215: Museum fur Vor und Fruhgeschichte, Saarbrucken, Germany/Bridgeman Art Library.

Religion Pages 217, 228, 231, 236, 242: The Art Archive/Archaeological Museum, Naples/Dagli Orti; page 218: Fitzwilliam Museum, University of Cambridge, UK/Bridgeman Art Library; page 221: Ashmolean Museum, University of Oxford, UK/Bridgeman Art Library; page 222: The Art Archive/Museo Nazionale Terme, Rome/Dagli Orti; page 223: Lincolnshire County Council, Usher Gallery, Lincoln, UK/Bridgeman Art Library; page 224: Arasta Mosaic Museum, Istanbul/Bridgeman Art Library; page 226: Ancient Art and Architecture Collection Ltd./Bridgeman Art Library; page 227: The Art Archive/Muzeul de Constantza, Romania/Dagli Orti; page 230: Louvre Museum, Paris/Lauros/Giraudon/Bridgeman Art Library; page 233: The Art Archive/Museo Opitergino Oderzo, Treviso/Dagli Orti; page 235: The Art Archive/Museo Prenestino Palestrina/Dagli Orti; page 238: Phillips, The International Fine Art Auctioneers, UK/Bridgeman Art Library; page 240: Origlia France/Corbis Sygma; page 243: Charles Plante Fine Arts/Bridgeman Art Library; page 244: Lauros/Giraudon/Bridgeman Art Library: page 246: Hadrian's Villa, Tivoli, Italy/Bridgeman Art Library; page 248: Scala/Art Resource, NY; page 251: Werner Forman/Art Resource, NY; pages 252, 256, 286: Araldo de Luca/Corbis; pages 254, 255, 262, 276: The Art Archive/Musée du Louvre, Paris/Dagli Orti; page 257: The Art Archive/Archaeological Museum, Ostia/Dagli Orti; pages 258, 264: Villa dei Misteri, Pompeii/Bridgeman Art Library; page 261: The Art Archive/Museo della Civilta Romana, Rome/Dagli Orti; page 263: Louvre, Paris/Bridgeman Art Library; pages 265, 268: Erich Lessing/Art Resource, NY; page 269: Mimmo Jodice/Corbis; page 270 top: The British Museum/HIP/Topham/The Image Works; page 270 bottom: Museo e Gallerie Nazionali di Capodimonte, Naples/Bridgeman Art Library; page 271: The Art Archive/Museo Civico, Trieste/Dagli Orti; page 273: The Art Archive/Dagli Orti; page 274: The Forbes Magazine Collection, New York/Bridgeman Art Library; page 278: Christie's Images, London, UK/Bridgeman Art Library; page 279: Galleria degli Uffizi, Florence/Bridgeman Art Library; page 281: The Art Archive/Galleria d'Arte Moderna, Rome/Dagli Orti; page 284: Musée Crozatier, Le Puy-en-Velay, France/Giraudon/Bridgeman Art Library; page 285: The Art Archive; page 289: Bargello, Florence/Bridgeman Art Library; page 290: Louvre, Paris/Peter Willi/Bridgeman Art Library.

ABOUT THE AUTHOR

Fox Gradin, Celestial Studios Photography

Kathryn Hinds grew up near Rochester, New York. She studied music and writing at Barnard College, and did graduate work in comparative literature and medieval studies at the City University of New York. She has written more than forty books for young people, most recently the four-volume series Life in the Medieval Muslim World. Kathryn lives in the north Georgia mountains with her husband, their son, and an assortment of cats and dogs. When she is not reading or writing, she enjoys music, dancing, gardening, knitting, and taking walks in the woods. Visit Kathryn online at http://www.kathrynhinds.com